The Polite World

The Polite World

A GUIDE TO THE DEPORTMENT OF THE ENGLISH IN FORMER TIMES

JOAN WILDEBLOOD

DAVIS-POYNTER
London

This revised edition first published in 1973 by
Davis-Poynter Limited
20 Garrick Street London WC2E 9BJ

ISBN 0 7067 0109 7

Printed in Great Britain by
Bristol Typesetting Co Ltd
Barton Manor St Philips Bristol 2

CONTENTS

ACKNOWLEDGEMENTS

Acknowledgements are due to the following: Messrs. J. M. Dent and Sons Ltd, for permission to quote from their Everyman editions of John Evelyn's *Diary*, Samuel Pepys's *Diary*, and *The Spectator*; Mr R. N. M. Murray for permission to quote from his translation of *De civilitate morum puerilium*, by Desiderius Erasmus, and for much valuable advice and assistance in preparation of the text.

Acknowledgements are also due to Evans Brothers (Books) Ltd for permission to use the quotations from *My Memories of Six Reigns* by Princess Marie Louise which appear on pages 25, 26, 175, 176, 179 and 194.

ILLUSTRATIONS

PLATES

ILLUSTRATIONS IN THE TEXT

AUTHOR'S NOTE

The manner in which an individual conducts himself in the established etiquette of his time has always been of importance in those circles in which attention is paid to what is regarded as correct upbringing. Fundamentally the basis of good manners is consideration for others, but all civilized societies have added to this basic rule various forms of social observances which are expressed both by word and demeanour, as when showing respect to others, or in greeting persons of differing age or rank. These have altered throughout the ages, and in the course of time old fashioned habits are no longer remembered. These ancient customs, however, should not be regarded merely as details of little consequence, for they are an expression of an age as much as the changes in dress or any other outward manifestation of a particular period. Today, on stage as elsewhere, prominence is given to the psychological aspect of characterization, but it does not always appear to be recognized that the outward forms of etiquette used among all peoples are in themselves an expression of this psychological aspect.

Some of the fundamental rules of etiquette, as observed during the periods from the fifteenth to the nineteenth centuries inclusive have been presented in *The Polite World* in the hope that they might form a guide to those to whom the matter is relevant.

At the present publisher's request this new edition of the book omits chapters 2, 3, 4 and 5 of the original edition, as in his opinion the contents should be confined to the deportment of various periods; he further requested that a brief description of the earlier Twentieth Century be included, rather as indicating a link between our own day and the past than as a comprehensive view of these later years. It is because of the omission of the above mentioned chapters, which, although I take responsibility for their inclusion in the first edition, were written by Peter Brinson, that the work now bears my name only as author. I would like here to acknowledge the help given to me by Peter Brinson who, in his capacity as a writer, gave me his professional advice in my preparation of the text for the chapters on the technical part of the work, where I put on record not only the substance of my research, but also the method by which I had previously taught these *manners in movement* over a number of years.

CHAPTER I

Period Deportment and the Stage

The Biblical Period

Of all the periods dealt with in this work the farthest away in time is the easiest to visualize. This is because the inhabitants of the lands of the Bible still retain in their way of life, and even in their dress, so much of what was customary in those far-off days. Studying the carvings and paintings of ancient Assyrian, Babylonian, and Egyptian artists, one can see men and women performing their daily tasks in the same manner as their descendants do today. Women carry bundles or jars upon their heads, perhaps holding a bird or two by the legs in one hand. Men hoist heavy containers of grain, wine, or other commodities upon their shoulders, or sit mending their nets, using their toes to hold the cord or string. They squat on the ground cross-legged (Plate IIa), or with their knees drawn up in front, enfolded in a sheet-like mantle (Plate IIb). They seem as oblivious of time as the people of the East today appear to the Westerner to whom speed is all-important.

The great courts of the Pharaohs and their satellites have vanished, but the impassive sculptures of these ancient monarchs and their subject-rulers still retain something of the power and majesty with which they awed their subjects. The humble prostrations made to these continue to be performed to some modern rulers. If the positions of two or more figures shown in Egyptian sculpture correspond to the placing of persons according to their degree in life, it would seem that the same principles were applied as in early European protocol. Where a Pharaoh is shown with his wife, he is placed on the right-hand side. If a queen is depicted with her daughter, the queen is shown on the right hand. Where there are three figures, the principal person is given the central position; the next in degree is placed on the right of the central figure, and the one of lowest degree on the left.

In general, we Westerners associate the peoples of the East with quiet, unhurried movements, and a traditional hospitality towards strangers. Greetings differ from country to country, but among certain nations of the East, and some Mediterranean peoples, the menfolk as well as the women embrace on special occasions as they have done for two thousand years. Ceremony in human relationships is still regarded as important. Occupations of daily occurrence, like buying and selling, and serving and eating food, are performed with due regard for correct etiquette.

In ancient times, there were few furnishings, goods, and chattels in the homes of ordinary people: the greater part of their lives was spent out of doors and houses were built more for shelter than comfort. Monarchs and men of great wealth received the servile attention of courtiers and slaves, to whom they behaved with autocratic condescension.

Medieval

Once the medieval ideals of good behaviour are understood, their theatrical application becomes inseparable from the management of costume. So static was medieval society in its human relations that we can be sure the early forms of this behaviour varied little from that which came to be recorded in the courtesy books of the fifteenth century after the invention of printing.

Styles of costume, for example, varied in detail from Norman times to the reign of Henry VII, but generally throughout these four centuries women wore long, flowing gowns, and head-dresses of which some types were more cumbersome than others; men wore variations of the tunic, hose, and long robe. Thus, from the point of view of *movement* on stage, the main consideration is the manipulation of flowing gowns, whose fullness and weight vary only slightly from one period to the next.

On stage the weight of material used for these robes depends largely upon financial resources. Student and amateur productions often have to be content with improvisations dictated by imperative economics, the effect of which can only be minimized by a knowledge of the correct period deportment. Good movement can better atone for a poor costume than good costume for poor movement. This may seem a truism, but players are not lacking who imagine that all faults will disappear with the donning of a costume.

The sense of weight can, and should, be conveyed in movement; in the turn of the body; in the manner of walking and even of sitting. This does not mean excessive *slowness* of movement, even for women. The poise of the head for men and women should be erect, the crown highest. If the head is tilted back, raising the chin, a heavy head-dress will cause a strain on the neck. Nor, for the same reason, should the head be dropped forward, even in a curtsy, apart from the fact that this also tends to conceal the face.

The train of the woman's gown should be lifted in the most practical manner required for the occasion (Plate IV*a* and *b*). The normal medieval practice of tucking the folds under the arm leaves the hands free for carrying things, and for gestures in conversation. Long and heavy sleeves do not lend themselves to fussy movements of the hands and arms. A sense of repose is desirable; it was deemed immodest for women to employ over-much gesture or, even in early times, to display their hands to excess.

When wearing a long train – and this applies to *all* periods – a lady who is obliged to turn back on her tracks should walk round the train, describing a semi-circle. When she is seated, the train should be arranged at one side of the chair. If no train-bearer is at hand to place the train conveniently, this can be done, firstly, by a turn of the body which assists in pulling in the folds of the train; then, if necessary, by drawing the train in with one hand, although such a practice was derided during the period of the farthingale. Obviously no player would bother with such matters when emotion becomes tense, but in the normal course of life and ceremony this is the rule.

Gentlewomen who acted as train-bearers tucked their own gowns under the arm, then looped the heavy folds of their lady's train over their arms (Fig. 1). This can be done only with trains which are very long and heavy.

Contemporary illustrations of women in medieval times

seem to show these ladies leaning backwards from the waist. As this would be an awkward and fatiguing posture, particularly in the garments then worn, it is probable that the weight of the body in walking tended to be pulled backwards owing to the drag of a heavy train and the thick folds at the back of the gown. The weight of the body, instead of its being carried over the leg which advances, tends to remain poised over the back leg.

In any play which requires a period atmosphere from medieval times to the nineteenth century, the body should be held very erect when walking or sitting in company (Plates IVa, VIb and c, X, XI, and XII). The furniture throughout these periods did not encourage lounging, nor was it considered good manners to behave thus in public. Although people were more relaxed in private, a lolling posture on the stage, generally speaking, is immediately suggestive of modern life.

The wearing of hoods, scarves, veils, heavy head-dresses, and high-necked garments tends to restrict the freedom of movement of the neck. To turn the head and body together – as if in one piece – naturally results from such a restriction. This habit then comes to be regarded as correct behaviour, cited, for instance, in the Knight of La Tour-Landry's advice to his daughter.[1]

In medieval times an outward and visible sign of the power of great and lesser lords alike was the grandeur of their household or court. The larger the number of retainers and the greater the attendant ceremony, the more they were held in respect by the people within their confined world. Thus monarchs and their nobles were surrounded by a mode of life in which every daily incident was attended by much detailed ceremony, such as the obeisances made to all persons of rank, according to degree. To enter or leave the presence of such persons without due ceremony would have been unthinkable (Plates V, VI, and VII). On stage this should not mean that a play's action need be held up by such points of etiquette, any more than the flow of a sentence is arrested by commas. The bow, the curtsy, the kneeling respect of homage – these punctuated naturally the life of polite circles. And such

[1] Early English Text Society (Original Series 33): *The Book of the Knight of La Tour-Landry*, Thomas Wright, London, 1868.

obeisances were made by individual to individual; it was not customary for a whole assembly to bow or fall upon their knees at the entrance of royalty. The assembly would rise to their feet, of course, if seated. As individuals, when passing a king or someone of royal blood, they would make a bow or curtsy. Although it was customary to make these obeisances in approaching someone of high rank (see p. 59) it is better to restrict these to two on stage, one on entering the presence, and one near the great person.

While it seems that the man's bow of the knee in medieval times was often performed without any inclination of the body, it usually looks better on stage if the man inclines his body slightly forward as one leg is carried backward. This does not apply to the full genuflection upon one knee; here the body should be kept erect. A general fault on stage is to drop the head too low. The recipient of the mark of respect should always be able to see the face of the person who makes the reverence.

When making the slight curtsy, the woman should keep her feet and knees together, then gently bend the knees while inclining the body and head only a little forward, as it were, in one piece. The gown can remain under the arm during this small curtsy, but for a deeper, more respectful reverence, the arms fall to the sides, and the gown slips from under the arm or the hands. All reverences, in any period, should be made without any appearance of haste; the greeting's significance may be likened to the modern handshake. Quick 'bob' curtsies belong only to those who expect no response – as a servant's in reply to some command. The correct way to complete the action of kneeling on both knees, made by women on occasions of importance, is to move one foot a half-foot's length behind that which carries the weight of the body; then to sink down, keeping the body as erect as possible, as if about to sit on the heels. When the knees come to the ground the weight should be taken on them, kneeling upright in the same action. Never sit back on the heels (Plates Ib and VIc).

If two persons of differing rank walk together, and it is convenient for stage or screen purposes to follow what used to be the correct etiquette, the one of inferior rank or age should keep a pace behind, with the point of his, or her, right

shoulder in a line behind the point of the superior's left
shoulder.

There seem also to have been fashions in facial expression
from one period to another. What medieval persons seem to
have understood by a 'sad' or 'sober' countenance was the
expression of a serious turn of mind, as opposed to someone
whose jocular behaviour may have concealed an empty head.
This deprecatory attitude towards laughter persisted for many
generations and sounds strange today. But it can be understood if it is realized that courtly behaviour sought to apply a
corrective to much that was uncouth and boisterous in a hard
and untutored age. In the fifteenth century, when portraits
were beginning to be painted, it is remarkable how many of
the sitters wear the same withdrawn, contemplative expression
shown in the faces of figures in religious paintings. It may be
argued that this was a contemporary fashion, followed by
artists of the time, but the ordinary citizen probably preferred
to have his likeness perpetuated in a manner approved by the
etiquette then in vogue.

The Sixteenth Century

Although the same principles of deportment continued from
medieval times into the first half of the sixteenth century, a
different attitude to demeanour began to be revealed in Elizabethan drama. The basic principles and rules of behaviour
remained unchanged, but there was a greater regard for the
individual expression of personality. Men chose fashions in
dress and copied patterns of behaviour which appealed to their
fancy. Thus they provided the dramatists of the day with
greater scope for characterization.

A man's figure was no longer hidden by long draperies.
Indeed, it was not hidden in the fifteenth century once the
outer robe was discarded to reveal hose and *jupon*. On and off
stage, the long hose looks unbecoming if not well pulled up
to avoid wrinkles (Plate VIII*b*). Where, too, the whole leg
is so revealingly displayed, attitudes in standing and the
manner of walking or moving assume a special importance.
An unintentional shuffling gait, bent knees, or pigeon toes
distract the audience's attention from dialogue and situation.
Hence elegance of motion and grace of stance are essential.

They can be learned by correct exercise today just as they were when *The Book of the Courtier*[2] was written and when dancing, fencing, and vaulting schools provided a means for acquiring proper poise.

Similarly, a man's shoulders should appear to carry his short cape or cloak with a certain air. Hired capes in costume productions today often hang limp like a damp dish-cloth down the back. The best way to improve this is by adding some kind of stiffened lining.

Accessories such as gloves, neck-chains, and pomanders should be handled as if they were the player's own property, a part of his life. This applies particularly to the sword or rapier at his side. To carry a sword well (for a man of worth must defend his honour and his name) was practised from an early age (see Plate XIII*a*). How often on stage are these weapons made to look like useless batons, encumbrances hooked on (as indeed they often are) just in time for the dress rehearsal!

Low bows, when the back knee almost touches the ground, are only to be associated with extreme formality; nor is it correct to kiss the hand except on special occasions. A player may overdo this action only where satire is intended, or a certain type of character is made fun of in plays of the period. When bending the knees while making the bow, it is correct to bend the body forward to a greater extent than for the medieval bow. When kneeling upon one knee, however, the body should still be kept upright, as in earlier periods.

When a shorter train became fashionable on women's gowns about the middle of the century it became possible to control it without using the hands. By turning the body, the farthingale swings the skirts and train into place, unless, for some ceremonial occasion, a very long train is worn. Too much swaying of the skirts when moving or walking can be irritating to watch. Long, striding steps look inappropriate, while mincing, jerky movements lack dignity.

A very smooth walk, which requires some practice, can make the wearer of a bell-farthingale appear to glide along. At times this is very effective. Contemporary accounts of inelegant behaviour are useful for stage purposes as an indication

[2] Count Baldassare Castiglione: *Libro del Cortegiano*, Venice, 1528. Trans. by Sir Thomas Hoby as *The Book of the Courtier*, London, 1561.

of how people did in fact behave, for it is obvious that the ideal
was not always attained.

The wearer of any kind of hooped skirt, such as the sixteenth-century bell-farthingale, the eighteenth-century round
hoop, and the nineteenth-century crinoline, should exercise
care when about to sit down. The width of the skirts and
train, if worn, makes it necessary to allow sufficient space
between the player and the chair before the turn is made to
be seated. In order to keep the back as erect as possible, and
avoid missing the chair, it is best to slide one foot on its toe
beneath the chair. This foot can then take part of the weight
of the body, thus enabling the latter to be kept straighter, while
the back of the leg, by feeling the edge of the chair, indicates
its position. The foot can also guide the folds of the train
beneath the chair. This is not only convenient when space is
limited, but is easier for the wearer than if the train lies
wrapped round the feet, and it avoids the possibility of standing on the train if the wearer is required to rise suddenly. In
maintaining the very erect posture when seated, the body will
feel less strain if the knees are slightly separated while the feet
remain close together. When full skirts hid the legs, and the
body was encased in very long-waisted, stiffly-boned bodices,
this was the usual posture adopted by ladies of fashion (Plates
VIb and c, XIa, c and d, XIIa and XVb).

On stage, the most common misuse of the fan is to flutter
it constantly, as though fanning the face. Naturally this was
the main purpose of the fan, but it was necessary to use it in
this way only if the atmosphere was close, or the owner felt
hot, or was fanning flies away. When used as an aid to natural
gesture, the fan can be very expressive. As this requires
practice, a fan should be made easy to manipulate since one
which is stiff to open and shut is useless. In the sixteenth
century the fan was often circular in shape and mounted on
a stick, but whether shaped in this style or that of the later,
folding fan, it should never be hung from the wrist by a cord
or ribbon; it was usually attached to the waist of the dress
by a cord.

Accessories, such as fans, pomanders, decorative handkerchiefs, chains, lockets, veils, masks, and so forth, can go far
to make or mar a part, depending on how they are used.

Mannerisms should be made to fit each character. A set style, applied to all occasions and roles, under the impression that it is 'Elizabethan' or any other period, creates a false atmosphere, which damages individual performance and the production as a whole. In real life no two persons have identical mannerisms, hence the palpable falsity of a set stage style, which so often sends audiences to sleep. This pitfall for students of drama is difficult to eradicate when once learned.

In all periods when it was customary to greet a friend with a bow or a curtsy, and where the scene includes spoken words of greeting, the action and the words should be performed *together*.

In medieval and Tudor plays servants are often produced with too little regard for the deportment and manners applicable to persons of their status. The so-called 'servant' who waited upon members of the aristocracy was not a low class menial but a member of the same class. Hence their bows and curtsies would be aristocratic rather than the awkward actions of simple, unpolished labourers. The apparent familiarity of dialogue between servants of good family and their masters (who were not always of high degree), is some indication of the true relations that existed in the domestic sphere.

The Seventeenth Century

It is not easy to convey a clear-cut picture of deportment style from the seventeenth century. In the opening years Tudor influence still prevailed; the age of the Stuarts witnessed a transition. This development was arrested during the Commonwealth by the temporary eclipse of the Court, and by Puritan inhibitions. Later, during the reign of William and Mary, deportment characteristic of the eighteenth century was already being practised.

Dramatists, moreover, from Ben Jonson to the Restoration playwrights, were fond of ridiculing behaviour which was familiar enough to their contemporaries, but is incomprehensible or merely boring today. The producer or actor in a Comedy of Manners will find, therefore, that a knowledge of the deportment of the period gives a better foundation upon which to create these characters, and that such knowledge explains the dramatist's wish to ridicule certain fashions of behaviour. Even if this is not as telling to the modern as it was to a contemporary audience, a certain wit and liveliness is lost if the nuances are not understood.

National characteristics loom larger in the literature and drama of the sixteenth and seventeenth centuries than before. The Englishman's love of aping foreign fads and fashions during this period affords the actor interesting scope. In playing the part of an Englishman who delights in giving himself French airs, the actor can use reverences and gestures suited to the Gallic style. Opposed to this is a style of behaviour associated with Roundheads or Puritans, about which there is a good deal of confusion. Puritans should not be regarded as mere boors. Their manners should conform to the prevailing custom, but be subdued in tone and without flamboyance.

The letters and memoirs of ordinary men and women of culture give a different impression of seventeenth-century manners from that portrayed by many of the dramatists, who concentrated upon the Court. The impression seems substantiated in the stolid portraits and homely scenes painted by artists of the period. So far removed are these from the wooden artificiality of Tudor likenesses that, were it not for their clothes, their subjects might be the men and women around us today.

The new naturalness was reflected in the teaching of deportment, where a 'seeming negligence' was said to be becoming. This did not mean the negligence of courtesies undone. On the contrary, the etiquette of the seventeenth century was more precise than ever, but the manner of performing the courtesies had to exhibit such ease of manner as to appear natural. The ease was found not merely in correct physical bearing, but in the way clothes were *worn*, and in the correct way of entering and leaving a room. All such details lend a flavour to a period, and are especially important from the later seventeenth century onwards, when dramatists begin to concern themselves more with ordinary people and their way of living. How to greet guest or host; to know the right bow or curtsy on specific occasions – these accomplishments should be made to appear as natural in the actor as they would have been in the persons depicted. They constitute the silent language of those bred to such behaviour, and the player can, and should, convey the impression that he, or she, has lived with these fashions throughout life.

The dress of a lady of Charles I's period feels almost modern in comparison with the weighty or stiffened garments of earlier periods (Plate X*b*). Herein lies some danger. The bodice or corset worn under the dress should be firmly boned and tight-fitting. As this is seldom reproduced in hired costumes of moderate price, the effect has to be achieved by the upright posture of the body, which must be maintained not only when sitting or walking, but in such a manner as to suggest a stiffened bodice in whatever movement is used – but without exaggeration. Head-dresses now were out of fashion, so the head, or rather the neck, acquired a freedom hitherto unknown in western dress. If the scene depicts a lady entering from the street or elsewhere, and the occasion is informal, such as entry into her own house, she could remove the hood and mask and unpin her tucked-up gown, after entering. If it is into the room of someone of high rank, these things should be done before coming into the room.

Among ladies of the Court, affectations of behaviour were said to have been demonstrated even in their manner of walking. In the old days, wrote Richard Brathwaite, women 'had not the art of imitating such huffing and mounting gaits as our light-spirited dames now use'.[3] Some, he says, gave the appearance of puppets in mechanical motion; others moved with haughty deliberation or, again, as though they were pacing the boards of a stage with affectation. He speaks of some who walked with a 'circular gait, as if they were troubled with vertigo': the implication being that they desired to appear grander than they really were – a pose brought out in Restoration comedies.

The Eighteenth Century

Evidence from numerous treatises on genteel behaviour, memoirs, letters, and, not least, contemporary portraits and conversation pieces, all confirm that eighteenth-century society as a whole acknowledged a common pattern of behaviour in

[3] Richard Brathwaite: *The English Gentleman*. London, 1630.

matters of deportment. The very erect posture, the hat placed under the arm while the hand is slipped inside the unbuttoned waistcoat; the fan held in poses advocated by teachers of deportment – these are examples (Plates X*d* and *e*, XII*a*, and XV*b*).

The dancing masters of the period, mainly responsible for tuition in good deportment, did not invent the attitudes they taught their pupils. They followed the conventions of their time, and guided those who required their assistance. It is certain that the majority of their youthful pupils would learn the same principles from their parents.

It is not sufficient, however, for a modern actor merely to study portraits and illustrations of the period. Sometimes the period image can be shattered by a player who consciously adopts poses taken from contemporary illustrations but who, in moving between these poses, fails to maintain the correct period deportment. He has not understood the motivation which created the poses.

The inclination of smart society in this period to live in towns like London or Bath, rather than on their country estates, created a type referred to by contemporary satirists as the Town Gallant and the Town Miss. These persons, no longer busied with their estates and country mansions, frittered away much of their time in coffee houses and the playhouse. Here are the gossiping fops and affected dames presented in the plays of Sheridan, and in the sundry tracts, memoirs, and letters in *The Spectator* and *The Tatler*. The ladies of the French Court who 'thought it ill Breeding, and a kind of Female Pedantry, to pronounce an hard Word right', are satirized by Sheridan in the person of Mrs Malaprop. So too, her idle, sensation-loving niece, Lydia Languish, bored by having too little to do.

A central place in many plays of the period was given to the Fop. His preoccupation with appearance doubtless stamps him, but stage fops often seem monotonously alike, and the movements adopted by players of this character are too reminiscent at times of a Harlequin.

Occasionally a production set in this period seems to call for treatment akin to the age-old tradition of the Harlequinade; not in the use of posturing, but by being played with a sense of lightness, as though the characters were too unreal to persist. Much of the effect would depend upon a sure touch in deportment. There should be, in any case, a lighter feeling in the deportment and movements of the period. The weighty garments and gravity of demeanour of earlier times give place to light satins or silks and sophisticated behaviour. Lengthy, heavy speeches are replaced by short, witty sentences. A sense of lightness should be expressed through the whole body: in the elegant use of the hands toying with a fan or snuff-box; in the turn of the body; in gestures used in conversation; even in the walk. The poise of the body is conditioned by the higher heels worn by both men and women, which help to carry the weight forward on the advancing foot when walking. High heels tend to shorten the stride, adding quickness and lightness to the step.

While the dress of men and women in the eighteenth century was light and easy in comparison with former fashions, the body was subjected, nevertheless, to inconveniences such as tight-corseting, awkward hoops or panniers, and elaborate hair styles for women; and for men, close-fitting knee-breeches, cravats, and wigs. Neither did the cut and setting of the sleeves in a garment give the freedom to the arm that is found in modern tailoring. It was said in those days that the first requisite of good movement was the knowledge of how to stand still. Great attention was paid to this, and a graceful stance shows off the leg, attired in knee-breeches and stockings, to better advantage than if the player adopts a posture more fitted to a ploughboy (Plates Xd, and XVb).

The normal interpretations of age, youth, and idiosyncracies of character have to be considered on stage, of course, in addition to the straightforward portrayal of period style. Whereas the young should make their bows and curtsies according to the correct mode, the aged would not be expected to be so agile nor so subservient in behaviour. To royalty, deep bows and curtsies should be made; otherwise it is a mistake to make these too low, or too ponderous. In greeting and leaving friends, reverences should not be overdone, nor ignored. Slight bows and curtsies should pass between persons as an acknowledgement of a compliment, or of some service done. On the stage, a bow or curtsy is often shown wrongly as a *movement*, rather than an *expression of feeling*. If the modern handshake were accompanied with as little expression of emotion as is shown in these stage reverences, it would appear offhand.

The Nineteenth Century

In a sense an understanding of background atmosphere and social circumstance is more important in portraying the nineteenth century than any other period, because the time is so close to our own. What separates us from them is mental outlook rather than physical behaviour, a nice distinction which can be represented on stage only by conveying the mind of the time.

Already by the beginning of the century the elaborate bows and curtsies, the protocol regarding the correct chair or position in which to sit, with many other details of earlier etiquette, were no longer needed. Behaviour on stage must reflect conduct which was then considered to be 'gentlemanly' or 'lady-like', and this usually emerges with the character being portrayed.

At functions such as balls, dinner-parties, and the paying of social calls, there remained an established etiquette. As a rule there is not much use for such observances in stage productions, though they can be valuable in films. The detail necessary on stage concerns rather the holding of hats (for example during a visit) and the etiquette of parasols; whether one should shake hands, or bow; and the right way to perform these actions. In plays set during the first half of the century, ladies continued to use the curtsy in polite society. In time, the slight bowing of the body which accompanied this curtsy was retained as a gesture of greeting, while the bending of the knees was discarded. The man's bow, now only a slight inclination of the body, was used more frequently – for example, when inviting a lady to dance.

For children, many little volumes on good behaviour were written with a markedly sanctimonious air. In these, the moral duty of children to those around them takes the place of advice on how to bow, curtsy, or take off a hat. For all their good intentions, these works contain a curious blend of piety and priggishness. But that manners constitute more than a mere formality of behaviour is emphasized by at least one of them, *The Child's First Book of Manners*. 'The subject of Manners is acknowledged by all to be of great importance,' says the Preface, 'and the wisest have agreed, that not merely the power of pleasing, but influence in society may be affected by the external demeanour. There is, however, a difficulty in giving instruction to children on this subject; for if we lay too much stress on mere outward polish, we may lead them to suppose that it is of superior value to the cultivation of right disposition.' Later, a final precept returns us to the fundamental simplicity which remains the basis of true politeness today, as it was in medieval courtesy. 'Some readers may think it strange to intermix religion with lessons on politeness; but for that no apology will be offered, since example may be taken from the divine record, and an inspired witness has given the precept, "Be ye courteous".'[4] It is this, indeed, which underlies all the ideals of polite behaviour evolved by society for its protection and elevation. To comprehend them is to comprehend the motivation of gesture and deportment, salutation and etiquette which formed so important a part of this society.

The Twentieth Century (1900–1929)
The principal forms and rules of polite behaviour formulated in the late nineteenth century, to suit more 'modern' trends, altered only superficially during the first fourteen years of the twentieth century, although those who knew these years would find various habits and fashions which, in their view, appeared to be either old-fashioned or up-to-date.

The most notable change in middle- and upper-class circles was the difference in outlook concerning women's role in society. At first only a small proportion of women were responsible for bringing their views to public notice, but their efforts to achieve greater recognition in worldly affairs, together with the changing attitudes towards education for girls and women, both scholastic and physical, started a movement which gained momentum up to the 1914–18 war: 'Then came 1914, and all was changed', wrote Princess Marie Louise (1872–1956), grand-daughter of Queen Victoria, in *My Memories of*

[4] Anon: *The Child's First Book of Manners*. London, c. 1860.

Six Reigns (1956). In these reminiscences of her youth, she observes that the view then held that certain behaviour was just 'not done' was constantly brought to the notice of the young by their elders, in spite of which 'our youth was gay and carefree'. Once, when talking to a group of young people of today, she told them that she grieved that in the strain and turmoil of modern every-day life they had never known what she could only describe as the graciousness of life as she knew it. This may be said to be one of the outstanding differences between the polite society of Yesterday and Today. The anciently named *Books of Curtesye* have in this present age become *Rules of Etiquette*, and the difference between the two is manifest. In the latter, little is said about the 'outward bodily meaning' in a person's deportment: what mattered was that they should know the *rules* in order to avoid being given the cold shoulder.

Graciousness of being and living is incompatible with constant hurry; a sense of leisure is an indispensable quality of its nature. Deference to the god of speed casts its influence over most events in modern life; this article and that (as in packaged commodities of all kinds) advertise the *saving of time* in their use. In the design of clothes which have become increasingly easier and quicker to put on and take off, laced-up corsets, layers of petticoats, innumerable buttons on dresses, gloves, and boots of former times, have mostly been replaced by fastenless pull-ons. Ladies' hats and gloves, once adjusted with the care almost of a ritual, now take but seconds to pull on, if worn at all. Men's dress likewise has changed in favour of ease and practicality.

Small matters of every-day life emphasize the relentless dominance of speed. Prior to the 1939–45 war, passengers wishing to alight from a London bus waited until the bus stopped at their destination before rising from their seats; the rush and bustle of the city's streets now necessitate traffic being on the move as much as possible – a legacy, also, of war-time conditions – so passengers have nowadays to rise to their feet in advance and stand swaying uncomfortably, ready to spring off the vehicle the instant that it stops. The clock appears to be the master now.

CHAPTER II

Medieval and Gothic

(a) DEPORTMENT AND ETIQUETTE

MEDIEVAL

'By the outward bodily meaning is oft known the inward disposition of the soul.'

Thus the bye-laws of their houses guided thirteenth-cen-
tury nuns in the ways of a disciplined restraint which
was reflected in all their movements and manners. But it
was not ecclesiastical orders alone which drew their disciplined
behaviour from such monastic regulations. The regulations, the
attitude, the visible conduct, became a model of good manners
also for the laity. It reflected the inward disposition of the soul
of all medieval society, the significance and purpose of all its
movements and manners.

When walking, women should move at an even pace, not
too fast; the shoulders, arms, and hands should not be thrown
about, nor should they 'look about too busily', but, keeping the
eyes 'somewhat down to the earth', assume an air of meekness.[1]
When going to town or to church, wrote a citizen of fourteenth-century Paris to his young wife,[2] she should be suitably
accompanied by some ladies of her household, for no ladies of
rank or good family ventured out of doors alone. She should
carry her head upright, but her eyes low 'without fluttering', so
that they were directed to the ground 'about four rods ahead'.
She should not allow her glance to rove around, nor stop to
speak to persons casually encountered on the way. And the
good wife's voice followed her daughter as she stepped out of
the house, warning her to beware of turning her head 'hither-

[1] Coulton: *Life in the Middle Ages*, Vol. IV. C.U.P., 1930, p. 320.
[2] Eileen Power: *Medieval People*. Penguin, 1937.

ward or thitherward' as she went, or from going a-gazing from
house to house.

Noble persons while in church were to forget the glory and
'bobaunce' of this world, bearing themselves with a suitable
stillness, 'for the Lord saith "Mine house is a house of beads"'.

> When thou art in the church, my child,
> Look that thou be both meek and mild,
> And bid thy beads.[3]

Quietness of bodily gesture at all times was a precept of
monastic tuition. So monks must be examples to others, for
priests, it was said, were the eyes of the world. When walking
out of doors they should keep their hands folded before them.
At divine service novices should stand straight, the hands held
inside their mantles or cowl sleeves, not shifting from foot to
foot, nor leaning against things, nor cupping their chins in their
hands. They should sit with upright posture, the legs not
stretched out too far, nor one knee crossed over the other, but
with the feet discreetly hidden under the clothes, the extremi-
ties of which should be drawn in close 'that they float not
abroad': and always, in places of silence, the hands should be
kept within the cowl sleeves.

Apart from this monastic teaching, the dress of the period
did not lend itself to unrestrained freedom of movement. The
long and heavy garments worn by fashionable men and women
of the fourteenth, fifteenth, and sixteenth centuries were easier
to carry with the hands folded in front of the waist, as is seen
in contemporary illustrations (Plates IVa, and VIIc). Just as
men today put their hands in trouser or coat pockets, so medieval man thrust his thumbs into the belt worn around the hips,
in an easeful, though hardly decorous pose (Plate IVc).

Extremes of any kind were to be shunned. In all things –
eating, clothing, speech – men and women should observe
the correct measures, or mean. 'Good manere in countenaunce'
and in their 'berynge' was expected from lords and ladies
whose example would be noted and followed by those who
looked up to them.

Women, in particular, were to be restrained in gesture

[3] E.E.T.S. (Extra Series 8): *How the Goode Wyfe taught her daughter*.
London, 1869.

and meek in manner. A too bold or affected manner was condemned invariably as belonging to a women of low morals.
Always in medieval ears were the words from Isaiah, iii, 16.

> *Because the daughters of Zion are haughty,*
> *And walk with stretched forth necks and wanton eyes,*
> *Walking and mincing as they go,*
> *And making a tinkling with their feet.*

And much quoted was the biblical picture of the good wife as
the mainstay of the household:

> *She looketh well to the ways of her household,*
> *And eateth not the bread of idleness.* (Prov., xxi, 27.)

The belief that idle hands caused mischief lingered well into
the nineteenth century. Even today it is quite usual for ladies
to take some form of embroidery when visiting friends informally. Medieval women seldom had their hands idle, but
worked constantly at the spindles and looms, besides doing
embroidery and stitching to beautify garments. This preoccupation with dress was one of the 'evils' frequently condemned
by churchmen of the time, and by parents who pointed out
the misfortune that this could bring. 'At the least excuse ye
weary yourselves with your garments; . . .' accused the
Franciscan preacher, Berthold von Regensburg, 'Ye busy yourselves with your veils, ye twitch them hither, ye twitch them
thither; ye gild them here and there with gold thread. . . . Ye
will spend a good six months' work on a single veil, which is
sinful great travail.'[4]

'Saint Paul teacheth how the good women shall attire them
when they . . . go to church,' said *The Book of Vices and
Virtues.* It elaborated the saint's views by emphasizing how
everyone must dress according to his position in life. A queen
would be expected to array herself in greater grandeur than
a burgher's wife, or the wife of a squire, or some other 'simple
lady, as a knight's wife'. Nor should women 'go with their
necks spread abroad as an hart in the land . . . looking . . .
over the shoulder as a proud horse of great price'. Widows
should live secluded lives, quietly with their maidens, without

---

[4] Coulton: *Life in the Middle Ages.* C.U.P. London, 1929. Vol. III.
p. 64.

thinking of the latest fashions in dress, but should be 'busy to do good deeds'.[5]

The Knight of La Tour-Landry, left with two young daughters to bring up, had much to say about their deportment. Tales of foolish maidens whose bad behaviour lost them favourable marriages appear to have been his strongest method of persuasion. One such was of three sisters. The first was fair to look upon, but was too frivolous in her manner. 'She looked small and winked oft, and spake before she understood what was said [to] her, and ever looked over the shoulder, and ever beating her eyelids together.' Another talked too much. She who was chosen to be wife of the king was not beautiful, but her behaviour won his heart, being demure and meek.[6]

The good wife taught her daughters that even when her husband got angry, 'look you meekly answer him'. She should not allow the rain to put her off from going to church; nor should she frequent plays or taverns. She must learn to keep her hands and feet still when sitting, and avoid showing her legs. Ribald jokes and loud laughter were not suitable for young maidens:

> Be fair of semblant, my dear daughter,
> Change not thy countenance with great laughter;
> And wise of manners look thou be good,
> Nor for no tale change thy mood;[7]

The importance of outward decorum was a constant theme of the classical world, which medieval writers quoted and elaborated. Good manners, wrote Cicero, arose from greatness of soul. 'In all our postures and gestures of body, such as standing, walking, sitting and leaning; nay, in our very countenance, in the cast of our eyes, and motions of our hands, we should be very careful to keep and observe what is becoming', avoiding the extremes of 'too much niceness and effeminacy' on the one hand, and 'clownishness and want of breeding' on the other.[8]

[5] E.E.T.S. (O.S. 217): *The Book of Vices and Virtues.* London, 1942.
[6] E.E.T.S. (O.S. 33): *The Book of the Knight of La Tour-Landry.* Thomas Wright. London, 1868.
[7] E.E.T.S.: *How the Goode Wyfe taught her daughter.* London, 1869.
[8] T. Cockman and W. Melmoth (Trans. 1753): *Cicero: The Offices, Essays and Letters.* Everyman, Dent, London, 1942.

Maidens were taught, in medieval days, that it was unbecoming to display too much curiosity, as might the untutored peasant who gazed open-mouthed at anything which caught his interest. When wishing to look aside, well-bred women did not look backwards over the shoulder by turning the head 'like the crane or the tortoise'. 'If you wish to look aside, turn your body and visage together.'

The Train of the Gown

The trailing, voluminous gowns worn by ladies of the court and the richer classes had to be lifted or looped up so that the wearers could walk. The skirt of the outer robe was lifted off the ground in front by tucking the folds under one arm. Not only did this leave both hands free for carrying things, but it would be less tiring than bearing the weight on the arm or in the hands, and was the accepted mode in courtly deportment. A medieval book on precedence declares that the train of the surcoat, gown, or mantle should not be too long in front, and should be trussed up under the girdle, or carried on the left arm. This appeared frequently in contemporary illustrations of court scenes. Women occupied as servants, or peasants working on the fields or farmhouses, have the kirtle tucked or pinned up behind, or at one side showing the under-robe (Plate IV*b*).

It was as bad manners for courtiers as for monks to allow the ample folds of their garments to 'float abroad', whether the wearers were standing or sitting, for this caused inconvenience to others. The length of the train on a lady's gown depended upon her rank; the higher the rank, the longer the train. These rules of precedence also affected the right of a lady to employ a woman instead of a man as her train bearer it being regarded a higher honour to have the train carried by a woman (Fig. 1). On occasions of special ceremony, kings, princes, members of the nobility, and churchmen wore long trains, and there were carried always by gentlemen of rank (Plate IV*d*). Women who delighted in wearing long trains on all occasions, says Erasmus, raised a smile, but for men, it was regarded as ridiculous.

The rules decreed that a duchess could have her train carried by a baroness so long as she was not in the presence of royalty, her estate being below that of the royal household. This rule applied throughout the degrees of nobility. If in the presence of a marchioness, a countess was denied the right to have her train carried by a woman; the same applied to a viscountess in the presence of a countess, and a baroness who was in the company of a viscountess. On these occasions, the lady had to be content to have a gentleman bear her train. At the lowest end came the knight's wife, who could 'have her kirtle born in her own house or in any other place, so it be not in her better's presence'.

Accounts of ceremonial processions of marriages and royal coronations confirm that this privilege of using women train-bearers, accorded to the highest ladies in the land, has been retained even to our own times, as was seen at the coronation of Queen Elizabeth II.

At the coronation of King Willian and Queen Mary in 1689, the king's train was borne by the Master of the Robes, assisted by four lords, and the queen's by the Duchess of Somerset and four ladies of rank. Queen Anne, at her coronation in 1702, clad in royal robes of crimson velvet, had her train carried by the Duchess of Somerset and three other ladies; while at that of George I in 1714, his train was borne by the eldest sons of four noblemen. George II and Queen Caroline, crowned in 1727, went in procession on foot from Whitehall to Westminster Abbey 'upon a Way raised for that Purpose, floored with Boards covered with blue Cloth, and railed on each side,' the king's herb-woman with her maids strewing sweet herbs before them. The lords in the procession carried their coronets and caps in their hands. The eldest sons of four noblemen carried the king's train, while that of the queen was supported by the Princess Royal, and the Princesses Amelia

---

PLATE I

a. The Duke of Edinburgh pays homage to Her Majesty the Queen at the Coronation, 1953, his hands between hers.
(P.A. – *Reuter Photos Ltd*)

b. A pupil of the Convent of Mary Reparatrix at Entebbe kneeling to Her Majesty in the manner of women in medieval Europe.
(P.A. – *Reuter Photos Ltd*)

a.

I. Attitudes of
homage practised from
ancient times to the
present day

b.

a.

b.

c.

d.

II. The ancient East

and Carolina, in purple robes of state, assisted by four other ladies. Princesses of the blood royal, such as the three present at the coronation of William IV, and again at that of Queen Victoria, had each a single lady train-bearer, with two gentlemen in attendance.[9] At the marriage of King George III to Queen Charlotte in 1761, the queen's train was carried by ten unmarried daughters of dukes and earls, and at their coronation her train bearers were Her Royal Highness the Princess Augusta, wearing her robes of state, assisted by six daughters of earls. King George's train was borne by six lords, the eldest sons of peers.

When dancing the more solemn, ceremonial dances at court, a lady of royal birth could have her train carried by another lady as she danced. This would not be difficult in a processional dance, such as the Pavane, which was sometimes used to open the ball.

Walking

When persons of differing rank walked together, the rules of precedence dictated how they should be placed. Where two persons only were concerned, the right-hand side was given to the one of highest rank, or one who deserved special respect.

[9] This was the case with Princess Margaret at the coronation of the present Queen. See Appendix II (b).

PLATE II

a. Votive statue of Ameny seated tailor fashion – a posture common today among Eastern peoples. Late XII Dynasty, about 2000 B.C.

b. Ka-mes, an official at the court of Amen-hetep III, seated with the cloak pulled round the arms and body, wearing a wig and beard sometimes seen on statues representing guardian or mourning figures. XVIII Dynasty, about 1420 B.C.

c. An unknown noble and his wife of the XVII Dynasty, about 1750 B.C. He is seated on the right-hand side.

d. Kneeling Pharaoh, Rameses II with offering table. Statues of kneeling figures are shown thus – sitting back on the heels, the body upright. XIX Dynasty, about 1320 B.C. (*Reproduced by courtesy of the Trustees of the British Museum.*)

C

FIG. 1   A woman carrying a Medieval lady's train (*British Museum*)

If three walked together, the centre place was the most honourable, the right-hand side came next, and the left-hand side the least. Customs varied in different countries; for example, in France the place of honour remained always on the right-hand side, if two were together. This is still the case in certain countries today. In England, however, when out of doors, the side next to the wall or hedge was given to those of higher degree or advanced years, as also to a woman today when a man walks in the street with her. In earlier times this position was the farthest from the filthy channels which ran down the centre of the street, and from the risk of being splashed by passing vehicles or horses.

According to Juvenal, the placing of the superior on the right-hand side was practised by the Romans. A work on good manners of thirteenth- to fourteenth-century Italy advises the reader to follow the usage of the country he is in. If, for example, a superior desired his companion to walk alongside, instead of one pace behind as was the normal custom between superiors and inferiors, good breeding enjoined that the inferior placed himself on the left, thus leaving the other's sword-arm free.

Cloaks and Hats

Should the superior be cloakless when it started to rain, the polite man would offer his own cloak. If this was declined, the owner of the cloak should refrain from donning it himself. The same applied to the wearing of a hat, for an inferior never wore his own hat unless his superior wore his, and invited the other to be covered.

When a man and woman walked together, the man gave the lady his right hand (Plate IIIc), thus placing her on the side of honour – often termed the 'upper' hand, or being placed 'above' the other. In this way an early French poem, *Le Chevalier à l'Epée*, drew attention to the fact that the host was, in manner, 'cortois' and not 'vilain':

> Li ostes, qui n'ert pas vilain,
> L'a prise par la destre main,
> Si l'a en la sale amenee.[10]

(her host, a right comely man, did take her with [his] right hand, and so did bring her into the room). (*Par* –*with*, as also *by*.)

Leading by the hand

The practice of leading someone by the hand, in the sense of performing a courtesy, is probably of very ancient origin. In the art of Sumeria and ancient Egypt, various scenes depict a 'dead' person being led into the presence of the chief deity. A limestone stele of about 20 B.C. in the British Museum shows the god Anubis (the jackal-headed god of the dead), leading

---

[10] Edward Cooke Armstrong (Ed.): *Le Chevalier à l'Epée. An old French poem. ll.* 263-5. John Murray. Baltimore, 1900.

a man into the presence of Osiris (Plate IIIa). In the papyrus of the scribe Ani and his wife, the god Horus leads Ani to Osiris.

In medieval times the same courtesy is frequently noted. It was retained as a mark of polite behaviour toward a lady until the eighteenth century, but it seems that medieval men observed the same courtesy between themselves. At the meeting between Richard II of England and Charles IV of France in 1396, the chronicler, Froissart, tells how the two kings having doffed their caps and saluted one another, 'took each other by the hand, when the king of France led the king of England to his tent; the four dukes took each other by the hand and followed them.'[11] The custom was noted frequently in ceremonial usage. When Henry, Duke of Lancaster was created king, the Archbishop of Canterbury, during the ceremony, knelt before the duke to make his address: 'The which, when he had ended, he rose, and, taking the duke by the right hand, led him unto the king's seat (the Archbishop of York assisting him), and with great reverence set him therein.'

EARLY SIXTEENTH CENTURY

Deportment in the early sixteenth century did not differ greatly from that of the later Middle Ages. The garments worn by both men and women were still long and full enough to restrict movement. The heavy folds of women's gowns had still to be carried though the introduction of stiffened petticoats gave more freedom of movement to the legs and feet.

Nicolo de Favri, who was attached to the Venetian Embassy in London about 1513, found the appearance and habits of English women interesting enough to describe to those at home who might be ignorant of this secluded island. 'In England,' he said, 'the women go to market for household provisions; if gentlewomen, they are preceded by two men servants. Their usual vesture is a cloth petticoat over the shift, lined with grey squirrel, or some other fur; over the petticoat they wear a long gown lined with some choice fur. The gentlewomen carry the train of their gown under the arm; the commonality pin it behind or before, or at one side. Their head-gear is of

[11] Jean Froissart: *The Chronicles of England, France and Spain.* Everyman, London, 1940. p. 558.

various sorts of velvet, with lappets hanging down behind over their shoulders like two hoods; and in front they have two others, lined with some other silk. Others wear on their heads muslins, which are distended, and hang at their backs, but not far down, but be the fashion as it may, the hair is never seen. Their stockings are black and their shoes doubly soled,[12] of various colours, but no one wears chopines, as they are not in use in England.' (Plate XVIf).

Englishmen, he continued, were 'well-made, tall and stout; well-clad, wearing gowns called doublets plaited on the shoulders and reaching half-way down the leg, and lined with several sorts of very fine furs', because 'in England it is always windy, and however warm the weather, the natives invariably wear furs'.[13] Thirty to forty years later, under Renaissance influence, the fashions of Favri's own Italy, together with those of Spain, began to make a greater impression in this island, where hitherto the prevailing influences had been those of France and the Low Countries.

Children

Children were taught to be 'in gesture and behaviour, comely'. Slouching, standing crooked, one shoulder higher than the other, was bad, said Erasmus, for 'young bodies be like unto tender plants which, into what fashion you bend them, so they grow'. Setting the arms akimbo, or crossed behind the back; thrusting the thumbs into the belt; running the hand through the hair, or cultivating the mannerism of tossing it backwards with a jerk of the head, were all frowned upon.

Spitting

Although spitting was accepted as a matter of course, it was expected that the well-bred would perform the act in the least disagreeable manner, children being told to hold the hand in front of the mouth when doing so. They should be well aware of where they spat, whether 'near or far'.

[12] Over-shoes, variously called shoes, pattens. Pantofles, into which the slippered feet were thrust, mostly when walking out of doors, appear to have been referred to in these days as 'double-soled' shoes.
[13] C. H. Williams: *England under the Early Tudors (1485–1529).* London, 1925.

Sneezing

Men of the ancient world believed that man's consciousness
and intelligence depended upon the lungs, and so on the
breath, and that, as the breath passed through the head by
the mouth and nose the head was, therefore, of particular
honour and holiness. This gave rise to the notion that the holiness of the head and the breath of life were in some way endangered by the act of sneezing. Hence, many nations have had
superstitious customs connected with sneezing. An ancient
Greek who sneezed said, 'Zeus save me', the Roman said
'Saluto'. The Jewish custom was to offer up a short prayer. In
the Bible the connexion between sneezing and life is shown
when the Shunamite's son, restored to life by Elisha, sneezed
seven times before opening his eyes.

Though these pagan superstitions were disregarded by the
orthodox Christian Church they continued to be observed,
and even recommended, in works of good manners for many
years. In the Middle Ages the words 'Christ help' were uttered
if someone sneezed, and were recommended by Erasmus. 'God
bless you', becoming 'Bless you', still remains with us as a
friendly exclamation. The notion, held by some, that it is
unlucky to reply 'Thank you' may have a link with this super-
stition of the past.

In addition to saying 'Christ help', adults and children of
the sixteenth century were supposed to remove their caps,
should someone sneeze. If sneezing themselves, it was polite
to turn aside, and afterwards to bless their own mouths with a
sign of the Cross.[14]

Laughter

Free, natural laughter, loud and uncontrolled, as might be
indulged in by rustic folk, was thought ill-bred by courtly
standards. The countenance, it was said in the sixteenth
century, should express mirth in such a way that the mouth
was not disfigured, nor the persons concerned bring upon
themselves the shaming reproach of a 'light mind'. Possibly
the poor, or even lack of, dentistry in those days may have
contributed to an unwillingness to reveal the teeth. Paul

[14] Eramus. *De civilitate morum puerilium.* 1530. Trans. R. N. M. Murray.

Hentzner,[15] writing in the sixteenth century, says that English teeth suffered from eating too much sugar, which caused many of them turn black. In the same period Italian ladies sometimes hid their teeth behind their fans when smiling.

(b) SALUTATIONS

ANCIENT WORLD

Salutation has always taken the form of the spoken word and the physical gesture, or most usually a combination of the two.

The Spoken Word

The natural reaction to an encounter with a stranger is one of caution; both parties being on their guard. Hence, among primitive peoples, suspicion and curiosity led to a series of questions and answers by means of which each learned the identity of the other. With the increase in civilized intercourse these questions and answers became woven into a formal mode of speech with which conversation was opened. Today, in the West especially, these formal introductions on meeting have become curtailed; in English we say only, 'How do you do?' But the lengthy inquiries concerning a man's family, his estates, and general well-being have not yet disappeared from certain parts of the world and, in fact, constitute a form of etiquette which is regarded there as indispensable. The departure of the stranger or friend called for the good wishes of all who bade him 'farewell', and what would be more natural than to send him off with the hope that his god be with him (good-bye).

The Hebraic salutation at meeting, recorded in the Old Testament, was that of a blessing: 'And, behold, Boaz came from Bethlehem, and said unto the reapers, "The Lord be with you". And they answered him, "The Lord bless thee." ' (Ruth ii, 4.) The Hebrew term 'Shalom' (peace) was related to general well-being.

The common form of greeting, either at meeting or parting, among the Greeks was ϱεχαι, the imperative form of the

15 Nichols: *Progresses of Queen Elizabeth*. Paul Hentzner's Travels in England during the reign of Queen Elizabeth. London, 1598.

verb meaning to be glad. In Latin *salve* ('hail' – from *salvere*, 'be well') and *vale* ('farewell' – from *valere*, 'be strong') expressed on the one hand the wish that the stranger might feel himself safe among friends and, on the other hand, that he would have strength to undertake his, perhaps dangerous, journey. These two wishes often merged, at parting, with the combination *salve atque vale*.

Western culture being predominantly influenced by the thought and literature of the Hebraic (Arab) world, of Greece, and of Rome, it is from these sources in the main that we discover the origins in our code of behaviour. The more ancient civilizations of Sumeria, Babylon, Assyria, and Egypt also affected the evolution of western conduct through their influence on all who came in contact with them, as in biblical times through trade with the inhabitants of the Grecian isles and peoples of the Mediterranean shores.

Physical Gesture. Obeisance paid to superiors

The attitudes and gestures used by the peoples of biblical times – Sumerian, Babylonian, Assyrian, and Egyptian – are depicted in the carvings, paintings, and the sculptures they have left to posterity. They are revealed also in the texts of prayers of supplication to their gods and kings. The worshipper, or the subject of the king, is shown either standing, kneeling, or prostrating himself before the deity or ruler. Prisoners brought before their conquerors prostrated themselves, their arms often tied behind their backs.

Egypt

In Egyptian art, in addition to the same three attitudes mentioned, is one depicting the subject standing with shoulders and back bowed in humility, both hands hanging near the knees, the wrists somewhat bent back so that the palms of the hands are parallel with the ground. The scribe Ani, coming before the god, assumes this posture, his left arm only held downwards, while his right appears to be holding his draperies on his left shoulder.

It seems from illustrations dating from the later dynasties that princes and priests bowed respectfully to the Pharaoh; servants threw themselves on their faces before the monarch.

Later representations also of the Pharaoh show the figure in the attitude of kneeling to make offering to the gods. The statuette of King Pepy I (VI Dynasty) is said to be the earliest known example of this kind. The kneeling postures of the Pharaohs and other high-ranking officials invariably show the figure sitting back on the heels, the knees close together and the toes curled under, leaving the balls of the feet on the ground. Sometimes the kneeling figure holds in each hand a jar, perhaps an offering of wine, oil, milk, or honey, his forearms and the backs of his hands resting on the thighs, the body and head held erect, and the eyes level. The attitude, though stylized, gives an impression of relaxation and simplicity, suggesting habitual usage. Sometimes these kneeling Egyptian figures hold an offering table with both hands (Plate IId).

The acts of bowing, kneeling, and prostration appear to have been performed by men and women alike. Some illustrations show women worshippers holding their hands in attitudes not seen in the male figures, but the posture of the body remains the same.

'I kneel, I stand, I seek thee', are the words from a Sumerian prayer to the moon god. And from cuneiform tablets found at Tel-El-Amarna, of the fourteenth century B.C. we read of the words of the suppliant addressing his king in terms of the physical homage paid to his lord: 'To the king, the sun, my lord, Abdasratu, your servant, the dust of your feet. At the feet of my lord, the king, seven and seven times I fall.' From the same source the fragments of two letters from a woman to her superior show that it was not to the Pharaoh alone that such expressions were used: 'To . . . my mistress . . . your daughter, your handmaid. At the feet of my mistress, seven and seven times I fall.'

Biblical

The books of the Bible confirm that the act of prostration to a superior, and even to an equal, was adopted by both men and women: 'And when the woman of Tekoah spoke to the king, she fell on her face to the ground and did obeisance' (2 Sam. xiv, 4). 'And, lo, while she [Bath-sheba] yet talked with the king, Nathan the prophet also came in. And they told the king, saying, "Behold, Nathan the prophet!" And when he

was come in before the king, he bowed himself before the king
with his face to the ground.' Sometimes the obeisance was
performed three times (1 Sam. xx, 41) and sometimes, as in
the meeting between Jacob and Esau, seven times (Gen.
xxxiii, 3).

Bowing with the face to the earth was the usual act in
worshipping Jehovah. In pagan worship the 'adoration' could
be performed, omitting the prostration and, instead, the hand
of the worshipper was carried to his own mouth and kissed to
the person, or object, of reverence: 'And my heart hath
been secretly enticed, or my mouth hath kissed my hand.' (Job
xxxi, 27.)

Prophets of the Old Testament testified that the enemies of
the Lord, or the king, should 'lick the dust' before him (Ps.
lxxii, 9, and Mic. vii, 17). Falling upon the knees in order to
hold the feet or knees of the revered persons was a variation
of the prostration.

Meeting between equals, Biblical

Apart from bowing the face to the earth, 'bowing the head'
or sometimes merely 'bowing before' a person is also recorded.
When David, the king, sent for Bath-sheba she 'bowed with
her face to the earth and did reverence to the king', but when
Solomon, her son, had ascended the throne and she came
before him to speak for Adonijah, Solomon 'rose up to meet
her and bowed himself unto her' (1 Kings ii, 19).

Between men, women, and even between the sexes, the
embrace and/or the kiss was the usual greeting, more particularly as a sign of friendship, or sometimes, of reconcilia-
tion, as when King David kissed his son Absalom. In his
ambition to supplant his aged father in the affections of his
people Absalom used this familiar form of greeting to all who
came to petition David. Placing himself by the entrance he
stopped those who were about to enter with words which
conveyed that, if he were able, he would see all men and
distribute justice: 'And it was so, that when any man came
nigh to him to do him obeisance, he put forth his hand, and
took him, and kissed him. And on this manner did Absalom
to all Israel that came to the king for judgment: so Absalom
stole the hearts of the men of Israel.' (2 Sam. xv, 5 and 6.)

This salutation of a kiss is frequently mentioned in books of the Old and New Testaments, and has been retained as a greeting of special favour amongst certain nations up to the present day.

Herodotus says that the Egyptians greeted one another in the streets, not by speaking but by making a low bow, dropping one hand to the knee. In Persia, he says again, they did not speak when greeting: equals in rank kissed one another on the mouth; one of slightly inferior rank kissed his superior on the cheek, and a man of much inferior rank prostrated himself in deep obeisance.

The Roman Emperor Diocletian (A.D. 245–313) assumed the attributes of royalty, and introduced to Rome much of the pomp and ceremonial he had found at the court of Persia. Whenever any of Diocletian's subjects, whatever his rank, was admitted to the emperor's presence, he was obliged to fall prostrate and to 'adore' him. The mode of adoration was said to be the respectful salutation of carrying the hand to the mouth in the kiss of reverence.

The nobles of his realm behaved, it was said, with arrogance, using terms of 'loud and insolent command'. Meeting those of their own kind they greeted them by an affectionate embrace, whereas others, less regarded, were 'not permitted to aspire above the honour of kissing their hands or their knees'.

Ancient Greeks

The Homeric poems show that the kiss of welcome was used by the ancient Greeks. At the reunion of a long-parted father and son, or master and servant, their joy overflowed in demonstrations of emotion, such as kissing the beloved's head, hands, face and eyes. 'And he came over against his master and kissed his head and both his beautiful eyes and both his hands, and he let a great tear fall.' (*Odyssey*, XVI.)[16]

Women displayed the same emotion towards those they loved. As Telemachus came to the house – 'the nurse Eurycleia saw him far before the rest, . . . and straightaway she drew

---

[16] Butchers and Lang: *Homer, The Odyssey*. London, 1887.

him, weeping, and all the other maidens of Odysseus, of the hardy heart, were gathered about him, and kissed him lovingly on the head and shoulders.' (*Odyssey*, XVII.)

Clasping the knees in supplication to kings and great lords

FIG. 2   Penthesilea, Queen of the Amazons, offers aid to Priam. William Smith: *A School Dictionary of Greek and Roman Antiquities*. London, 1845. (*British Museum*)

was a gesture of fear and gratitude (*Iliad*, Book 478). Clasping the hand as a gesture of friendship or as a pledge of honour is mentioned throughout the works of classical authors.

> *Thus as they spoke, they quitted each his car;*
> *Clasp'd hand in hand, and plighted mutual faith.*
> (*Iliad*, VI. 274-5).

To offer the right hand in welcome occurs in passages of the *Odyssey*. 'So he spake, and he came close to him offering his right hand in welcome, and uttering his voice spake to him winged words: "Father and stranger, hail!".' (xx.)

When Telemachus saw Athena standing by the outer porch, he went to her, 'for he thought it blame in his heart that a stranger should stand long at the gates; and halting nigh her he clasped her right hand and took from her the spear of bronze, and uttered his voice and spake unto her winged words: "Hail, stranger, with us thou shalt be kindly entreated." '

Romans

Amongst the Romans the right hand was extended as a pledge of honour and of friendship, as with the Greeks (Fig. 2). *Dextra* [*manus*] – the right hand, was figuratively used in this sense. *Dextram dat iuveni* (he gives his right hand to the youth), is one of many examples.

MEDIEVAL AND GOTHIC

The Spoken Word

A French-Flemish Grammar, thought to be of the first half of the fourteenth century, and later published by Caxton in a French-English version, contains some phrases of greeting and farewell used by medieval men and women. 'Sir, god you keep', was correct when saluting someone; 'that is the shortest that one may say'. Or perhaps, 'Sir, ye be welcome'; and 'Ye lady, or damoiselle, ye ben welcome'. Also, 'Sir, god give you good daye' and 'Fellow, or friend, ye be welcome'. The biblical form (in use in India today) of hailing another man as 'Brother' appears to be foreign to the speech of Englishmen.

To one who said 'I take leave of you', the answer was 'Our lord conduct you', or 'God have you in his holy keeping', or quite simply, 'Go ye to God'. The salutation 'God speed' was usual to those whom one met on the road, or encountered on entering a dwelling.[17]

17 E.E.T.S. (E.S. 79): Caxton, *Dialogues in French and English*. London, 1900.

Physical Gesture. Reverence to God

Medieval men and women did not prostrate themselves even in their religious worship. The nearest they got to the ancient, or Eastern, form of prostration was to kneel in prayer on both knees; but the body from the knees was held erect (Plate V*a*). The hands of the kneeling worshippers express the significance of their devotion. The head was sometimes bowed, sometimes raised in adoration, and in the eyes can be seen the withdrawn look of those who contemplate an inner vision.

Homage to an Overlord

The ceremony of a vassal paying homage to his lord took place when the former gave his oath of loyalty, and in return received the grant of a fief (feudal benefice). With his head uncovered, the vassal laid aside the accoutrements of war – his sword, spurs, and belt – and kneeling on one knee, he joined the palms of his hands together, extending them towards his lord who took them between his own, while the words 'I become your man from this day forth, of life and limb, and will hold faith to you for the lands I claim to hold of you', were spoken by the vassal (Plate I*a*).

Early English books of courtesy make clear the distinction between honouring God and honouring a human lord: 'Be courteous to God, and kneel down on both knees with great devotion. To man thou shall kneel upon the one, the other to thyself thou hold alone', and 'Kneel but on one knee to your sovereign or lord, whoever he be'.

The Bow

The transition of the bow from medieval to modern times is the gradual change from the action of bowing the knees to that of bowing the body. The medieval meaning of the term 'to bow' meant to bow the knee; it was immaterial whether or not at the same time the body was also bowed. The movement was a half-kneel, taking one leg backwards and bending both knees without touching the ground with the back knee (Plate V*d*). This semi-kneel was merely a curtailment of the full reverence when the knee touched the ground, and was used on occasions when the deeper bow was not appropriate. To touch the ground with the knee was usual before persons of royal or noble rank, or on certain occasions in order to convey particular respect. A Scottish ballad, 'Thomas the Rhymer', describes a meeting with the Queen of Elfland when 'True Thomas he took off his hat, and bow'd him low down till his knee'. (Another version gives 'louted low down to the knee'.)

In France and England it was customary to perform this bow by taking the right leg back, maintaining the tradition whereby the right-hand side indicated greater respect. Approaching a king or a noble lord, the bow was made two or three times, the first just inside the entrance hall or room, the second midway, and the third close by the king: 'Twice or thrice without doubt to that lord thou must lout. With thy right knee let it be done.' Likewise when leaving the presence of such a person the same action was used, either once or twice. Instructions to a page, squire, or any servant in the household of a noble lord were that 'ever when ye depart from your sovereign, look ye bow your knees'.

This constant genuflecting and kneeling down had an effect on men's hose that is not surprising:

> To you that O'er the whele [weald]
> Great lords must crouch and kneel,
> And wreak their hose at the knee,
> As daily men may see.
>   *Colyn Cloute*[18]

Neither was the action easy for the fashionable gallant who wore his hose so tightly braced that when he tried to bow or kneel he was obliged to move his leg round in a circular motion – 'in the manner of a windlass' – and could scarcely bend his body for fear of a lace in doublet or hose breaking.

Doffing the Hat

The doffing of the hood, cap, chaperon, or hat was part of the bow and either preceded it or was simultaneous with the

[18] E.E.T.S. (O.S. 32): In *Early English Meals and Manners*, 'Additions and Corrections,' London, 1868.

action of bowing. To remove the covering of the head has been and is still a token of respect in the West, while in the East the corresponding action is the removal of the shoes.

Doffing the hood consisted in pushing it back off the head, and if it was not pulled on again at once it was left hanging at the back. The cap, or hat, was held in the hand, either down by the thigh or in both hands in front of the body, the inside of the cap towards the body. Some held their caps under one arm, but in medieval times it was not fashionable and was even considered to be a 'rudeness'. When the chaperon with the long scarf attached was worn, the headpiece, after removal, was thrown back over the shoulder, leaving the scarf draped over it; the scarf could then be kept in position by placing the end under the arm, pressed against the body, or by holding it in the hand.

Women. The Curtsy

The women's curtsy followed the same principle as the man's bow. She bowed the knees, an action which she performs to this day on occasions which demand this courtesy. Her movement was considered to be the same as the man's, whose bow was referred to also as a 'curtsy' until the time of Shakespeare. Illustrations of the period, however, show a notable difference between the man's and woman's full reverence when the knees touched the ground. For whereas the man knelt on one knee to a person of high rank, the woman is shown always on both knees (Plates VIc and Ib).

Today, wherever this form of respect is still used, it will

PLATE III

a. Limestone stele of the Roman period, 20 B.C., showing the god, Anubis, leading a dead person into the presence of Osiris. (*Reproduced by courtesy of the British Museum.*)

b. A marriage feast, seventeenth century. Here the groom takes the right-hand side, as is our custom today, indicating that he is head of the house. *David Teniers.* (*Reproduced by permission of Mr Edgar Ivens.*)

c. The Fair of Ghent, in the seventeenth century. The Gentleman leads the lady with his right hand; the page follows. A good example of the contrast between studied deportment and the natural behaviour of the crowd. *David Teniers the younger.*

a.

b.

c.

III.   The custom of leading another by the hand

a.

b.

c.

d.

IV. Managing the train

be seen that the knees, in bending together, touch the ground simultaneously, or almost so, while the feet remain close together. It is natural, therefore, that the beginning of the movement, when the knees start to bend, constitutes the curtailed form of the woman's full reverence, thus making her less formal curtsy. These two forms were used in old Chinese etiquette according to a lady-in-waiting at the court of the last empress – the 'kow-tow' and a slight bending of the knees used to those of rather inferior rank. A courtesy book of the early sixteenth century suggests that though this movement of slightly bending both knees together was used by both sexes, it was used more by women than by men.[19] In matters of this nature custom changes slowly and that which was remarked upon at this date could easily have remained from an earlier period. Moreover, the practice of keeping the feet together while bending the knees continued in vogue for the woman's reverence till the end of the eighteenth century.

The lady doffs her hood

When out in the street or riding on horseback women covered their heads with a hood, as did men. Possibly because this concealed much of the face (and it was ill-mannered to hide the face when meeting anyone) there are references to women doffing their hoods when greeting someone. If 'ladies and demoiselles' doffed their hood, 'set it on again with your

[19] Eramus. *De civilitate morum puerilium*. 1530. Trans. R. N. M. Murray.

PLATE IV

a. Medieval. A lady holding her gown under the left arm in accordance with the usual practice. (*Roman de la Rose, c.* 1500.)

b. Medieval. One lady lifts her skirt; the other has hers tucked up in the manner often used by servants. (*Roman de la Rose.*)

c. Medieval. One way of tucking up and securing a long train at the back of the gown. Note manner of wearing chaperon with scarf, and the low belt (with purse and dagger) on which the hand rests. (*Roman de la Rose.*)

d. Seventeenth century. A Royal procession, with gentlemen's robes carried (with little display of ceremony) by gentlemen train-bearers. *Abraham Bosse.* (*Reproduced by courtesy of the Trustees of the British Museum.*)

D

hands' is the advice given in an English-French grammar of
the fourteenth century. And the book of La Tour-Landry en-
treating women to 'be courteous and humble to great and
small', relates to a tale of a great lady who doffed her hood
and bowed herself to a tailor. 'Madam', said one of her knights
in attendance, 'you have doffed your hood to a tailor', to
which she replied that 'she was gladder' that she had done
this to him rather than to a lord: 'And they all saw her meekness and wisdom, and held her wise.'[20]

Children

A small boy, not yet out of his youthful petticoats (Plate
XIII*a*) wore a hat or cap like all men and youths, and he
learned to doff it and to bow his knee as did his elders. In easy,
rhyming couplets the child was taught his manners:

> *When thy better speaks to thee,*
> *Do off thy cap and bow thy knee.*[21]

He also knew that he was not to replace it until told to do
so, and that he should perform these courtesies whenever
he came into, or went out of, the presence of those older or
superior to himself.

The daughters of the household carried themselves with all
the dignity of which they were capable, being both in appearance and behaviour like miniature copies of their mothers
and the other ladies of the establishment. Whether they entered
or left a room, whether they spoke or were spoken to, or if
they met anyone in the house or out of doors, they made
reverences in the same fashion as their elders.

Servants

As we have shown, royal and noble persons, both men
and women, were waited upon by lords, knights, squires,
pages and ladies-in-waiting, who often gave their services,
among other reasons, because of the prestige of being attached
to some household of importance. Children who were sent to

[20] E.E.T.S. (O.S. 33): *The Book of the Knight of La Tour-Landry*. London, 1868.
[21] *The Young Children's Book, c.* 1500. In *Early English Meals and
Manners.* E.E.T.S. London, 1868.

the establishment of some nobleman as a means of receiving an education also learned to wait upon their master, mistress, and other members of the house. In doing so they used the courtesies practised by all – that of bowing the knees, and/or of kneeling. This they did if called upon to serve a person, and only when their presence was noted in the carrying out of these duties. At other times those who served merely stood still, or moved quietly about without attracting attention to themselves. Thus, when John the Good, King of France, had concluded a treaty with Edward III and paid him 600,000 francs ransom for his freedom, he was entertained at Calais by the English king at a magnificent banquet in the castle: 'All was well arranged, and the children of the King of England, together with the Duke of Lancaster, and the most noble English barons, waited bareheaded. After supper the two kings took a final leave of each other in most gracious and affectionate manner.'[22]

The Embrace

The kiss of greeting was used among all persons as a demonstration of affection, of good will, or of bestowing honour, between men, women, and between the sexes. A father and son, or friends of equal or nearly equal rank, could embrace one another either when meeting after an absence of some time, or in taking farewell. If they were of unequal rank or age, the initiative came from the superior or elder. After the battle of Crécy where Edward, the Black Prince, had fought with great gallantry, his father, Edward III, in the words of Froissart, 'embraced his son and said to him, "Sweet son, God give you perseverance: you are my son; for most loyally have you acquitted yourself; you are worthy to be a sovereign." The prince bowed very low, giving all honour to the king, his father.'[23]

During the same reign, the wife of Jean de Montfort (who was claiming the duchy of Brittany and was at this time a prisoner of the French) paid honour to Sir Walter Manny who had been sent by the English king to assist her against Charles de Blois and the French nobles, who disputed her hus-

[22] Froissart: *Chronicles.* Everyman. London, 1940. p. 73.
[23] ibid., p. 49.

band's claim. Froissart, eager to record the military exploits
of his friend, Sir Walter, described how, after a skirmish
against the French, the victorious English knight was received
by the Comtesse de Montfort. She 'kissed Sir Walter and all
his party, one after another, like a noble and valiant dame'.[24]

The Handclasp

Strictly speaking, the joining of right hands between two
people should not be included among the usual forms of
salutation, for it was not a common act of greeting. As a
practice inherited from classical times, or earlier, it still held
the implication of a pledge of honour or of friendship (Plates
V*d*, and VIIc).

Queen Philippa, wife of Edward III, became patron and a
true friend of Froissart so it may be assumed that his account
of her death in 1369 was based on evidence, though he himself
was abroad at the time: 'When she saw her end approaching,
she called to the king, her husband, put her right hand into his,
and spoke thus: "We have enjoyed our union in happiness,
peace, and prosperity; I entreat, therefore, that on our separa-
tion you will grant me three requests." The king, with sighs
and tears, replied, "Lady, whatever you request shall be
granted." '[25]

During negotiations for a truce in 1396, Richard II of England and Charles VI of France met at the tented camp prepared for the occasion. Here 400 French and 400 English
knights were drawn up, brilliant in their shining armour 'with
swords in hand'. Passing between their ranks the two kings
met bareheaded, and, *having saluted*, took each other by the
hand, 'whereupon the eight hundred knights "fell on their
knees and wept for joy" '. Vivid and informative are these
details, however romanticized, in the words of the fourteenth-
century chronicler who had the opportunity to observe and
record so many momentous happenings in his day. The unknown miniaturist who illustrated a portion of the chronicles
in the fifteenth century, had ample choice of incidents on
which to draw. Yet the most frequent subject of his illustration
is that of persons kneeling, or sometimes bowing, and clasping

[24] ibid., p. 36.
[25] ibid., pp. 124–5.

hands with a king or a lord. In the fashion of his day the artist clothes his figures in the dress of his own period, and his little doll-like images bear no trace of attempted likenesses. It is sufficient that they represent the chief characters in the episodes in which they were concerned, where in real life they would have performed these same actions – actions which were a part of the symbolic ceremonial that accompanied important events, as the signing of treaties and giving of pledges of friendship and support. We see the English ambassadors and envoys kneeling before the king of France (Plate V*b*). We see the Archbishop of Canterbury, attired 'as a simple monk on a pilgrimage' bowing his knee before the Earl of Derby (Bolingbroke) while the two clasp right hands as a sign of mutual trust. The Archbishop had been sent to France secretly to persuade Bolingbroke to return to England to become king. 'In everything the greatest secrecy was observed: and the earl took leave of the king of France, under pretence of paying a visit to the Duke of Brittany.' Booted and spurred, the earl is shown kneeling to the king of France, their right hands clasped and, in the courtyard outside, as he mounts his horse on the first step of his journey to become, before long, king of England, he turns to clasp right hands with one of a group of courtiers who kneel, hats in hand, to give him farewell.

It belongs to history how Richard II plotted against his uncle, the Duke of Gloucester, in an action which at the time caused the dark murmurs against the king to multiply around him. 'Under pretence of deer-hunting' Richard arrived as an unexpected visitor at the ducal residence, Pleshy Castle. The miniaturist depicts the king, unrealistically wearing his crown, joining his right hand to that of the duke who kneels before him, for, says Froissart, the duke paid the king 'all the respect due to a sovereign, as did his duchess and her children'. Commanded by Richard, the Duke, unsuspecting, took leave of his wife and family and rode away with the king, never to see them again.

(c) HOSTS AND GUESTS

Most nations have regarded hospitality as a principal virtue. To turn away a stranger at the door – assuming it was known he was not an enemy – might bring ill luck. If news came that a prospective guest (or guests) was due to arrive, custom decreed that the host, perhaps accompanied by members of his household, should go out to meet him. The greater the honour to be conferred upon the guest, the further his host would travel. Humble folk hastened across the fields, or down the village street. Richer men used their discretion according to the rank or importance of those whom they welcomed to their house. To demonstrate particular honour, they might ride some distance from their estate; or it might be only to the gates of their domain; or even to the outer door of the house, or merely by moving across the room to give a greeting at the door, unless it was sufficient to rise up from a divan, couch, or chair, within the chamber used for receiving visitors.

With royalty and great personages, state etiquette regulated the precise distance to be covered. In royal households today, the distance is set by the site of the sea-port, railway station or air-terminal. All these forms have been regulated by custom, stretching back in time to the unfailing hospitality of ancient tribes and early civilizations.

A tired traveller, after a long journey in the hot and dusty countries of the Far, Middle, and Near East, needed water to refresh hands, face, and feet. In eastern countries the custom of changing into clean clothes before eating food continues to be observed today; and in ancient times, in addition to food and drink, the host often provided clean raiment for those who had travelled far. When all men wore loose garments of uniform style, this entailed no great difficulty.

Having seen to his guest's physical needs, the host would turn his attention to the refreshment of the mind, with entertainment in music, dance, and other spectacles of varying magnificence, according to his means. Guests, on their part, were expected to show appreciation of their host's hospitality, as Athenians did, by dressing themselves with greater care than usual when invited to a feast.

On arrival at a medieval castle or manor house, the visitor was met by a porter, or keeper of the door. From the porter he inquired whether he might see either the master or some member of the household. Depending upon the rank of the visitor, the porter would lead the guest to his master, or the host would himself come out to greet him.

Large medieval establishments kept open house for way-farers, many of whom were simple knights and squires who merited no particular honour when they arrived to enjoy the customary hospitality given and expected in those days. Courtesy decreed that such a person should make known his presence to the lord of the house. On being told that the master, usually with other members and guests of the household, was to be found in the great hall, the young man removed his gloves and hood before entering. Inside the door, where many people would be gathered, he paused an instant to make his first bow to the company in general, saying with an air of courtly humility, 'God speed', to all who were there. Advancing towards his host – with 'an easy pace' – he made further bows to those he passed on his way to the upper end of the hall, where the lord of the house might be seated on the dais. There, in exchange of greetings with the host, the visitor would fall upon his right knee, unless his host came forward to prevent this formal courtesy, or bade the young man rise and come to him.

Behaviour was regulated by rules of precedence, set forth in various Rules and Orders for royal and noble households.

Entering or leaving a room

Thus, all persons, of whatever age or degree, observed the courtesy of making a bow or curtsy upon entering or leaving a room where there were persons of either superior, or equal rank or status to themselves. This form of etiquette was observed throughout the years up till the early nineteenth century; the bow and curtsy corresponding to the mode of the day.

Kneeling

Similarly, the one of inferior rank knelt when approaching to speak with a superior, or in presenting or offering some gift, or performing a service such as giving food or drink (Plate Vc). During the Middle Ages and the sixteenth century, the servants of all large establishments performed this courtesy to their masters or superiors as a matter of course. In the

seventeenth century it continued in the ceremonial etiquette
of service to royalty. Today vestiges of these ancient customs
remain in the opening of Parliament and other State ceremonial.

Children

For many years the behaviour of children towards their
parents was of extreme formality. Meeting their parents in the
morning, children knelt to ask their blessing. They never sat
in the presence of parents or other grown-ups unless given permission, nor would they speak unless to answer a question. An
account, said to have been written in 1678, criticizes the
severity which parents used in earlier times towards their
children. 'The gentry and citizens had little learning of any
kind', said the writer, attributing the old attitude to lack of
education, 'and their way of bringing up their children was
suitable to the rest. They were as severe to their children as
[were] their school masters. . . . The child perfectly loathed
the sight of his parents, as the slave to his torture. Gentlemen
of thirty and forty years old were to stand like mutes and
fools, bare-headed, before their parents: and the daughters
(grown women) were to stand at the cupboard-side during the
whole of the proud mother's visit, unless (as the fashion was),
leave was desired, forsooth, that a cushion should be given
them to kneel upon, brought them by a servingman, after they
had done sufficient penance in standing. The boys (I mean the
young fellows) . . . were to stand mannerly forsooth thus . . .
with one hand at the band-string, the other behind the breech.
The gentlewomen had prodigious fans . . . with which their
daughters were oftimes corrected.'[26]

In ancient times and until it became the custom to employ
paid servants, children were expected to wait upon their
parents and guests of the house. Courtesy of this nature was
noted frequently in medieval and Renaissance literature.
Daughters of kings and noble lords performed almost menial
tasks, corresponding to the washing of the guests' feet by the
women of biblical times. So it was that the daughter of King
Leodogran and her maidens waited upon Arthur and his

[26] The Antiquarian Repertory: *MS. c. 1678 in Library of Thos. Astle.*
London, 1807.

knights. The shining armour of knights in all their glory was confined to the field, to jousts and feats of prowess. Only in the late sixteenth and the seventeenth century was part-armour worn in a decorative sense as an emblem of knighthood. The cumbersome armour of the medieval knight was an unsuitable, in fact impossible, garb in which to appear for the purpose of gentle, courtly entertainment. On arrival, therefore, a knight who was fully armed, would first be helped to remove his armour. On being rid of such weight and discomfort, the relaxation of a herbal bath (or 'stewe' as John Russell calls it) would be very welcome. Guests were given water for washing, as were the travellers of ancient times. In the romance of *The Prose Merlin*, King Leodogran commanded his daughter to wait upon Arthur and the knights of the Round Table. After their armour had been removed, they washed in warm water, brought in basins of silver by the king's daughter; the king then 'made his doughter to aray them in riche robes'. While the princess served Arthur, in washing and drying his face and neck, the steward's wife, with other maidens, waited similarly upon the rest of the company.[27]

State Receptions

The etiquette of state ceremonial was the same as that used in daily life, but with added grandeur and formality. It was not something unique as it has become today. Obeisance was made not only by vassals or servants of a great lord, but formed part of the ceremony used on occasions of state visits by one sovereign to another. This included the audiences given to visiting ambassadors who arrived to present their credentials to a monarch.

The three bows

The number of prostrations made when approaching a monarch, or high dignitary, has varied in different countries and ages. At the courts of ancient Egypt, Persia, and China, it could be from three to nine; at the feudal courts of Europe the customary number used on ceremonial occasions was three. The first of these was made just inside the doorway;

[27] L. Cranmer-Byng: *The Prose Merlin*. Selections. A Series of English Texts. Sidgwick & Jackson. London, 1930. p. 39.

the second about midway down the great hall, and the third close to the dais, or wherever the monarch or noble lord, was placed (Plates V*b*, and VII*c*). This ceremonial etiquette of the three bows to the sovereign has been retained at the English court to this day on occasions when an ambassador arrives to present his credentials. Naturally, the method of performing the bow has followed the practice of the day. The genuflexion used in medieval times has developed into the simple form now used (see Appendix II(*c*)).

Ambassadors

The records of ambassadors whose duties took them to the various courts of Europe often contain descriptions of the audiences they received. The exact manner in which the monarch received the ambassador was significant, because it reflected in outward form something of the political relationship between the two countries. The ruler of a country who desired an alliance with another, would be careful to accord its ambassador every courtesy, with all possible honour and entertainment, a fact duly reported by the ambassadors in their dispatches home. The smaller states who wished to advance their interests with their more powerful neighbours were particularly sensitive regarding the reception accorded to their representatives.

In April 1515, Sebastian Giustinian, the Venetian ambassador, arrived in England with his retinue. His secretary, Nicolo Sagudino, reports that King Henry VIII sent 'a prelate and a knight and an honourable train', to escort them from the house provided for them to the palace at Richmond. Assembled to greet them were 'the whole court, and well nigh all the lords and prelates of the kingdom'. On being ushered into 'a stately hall' where the whole assembly was gathered, they found the king standing near a gilt chair – 'covered with cloth of gold brocade, with a cushion of the same material, and a large gilt sword under a canopy of cloth of gold with a raised pile'. The king's robes consisted of 'a very costly doublet, over which was a mantle of violet-coloured velvet, with an extremely long train, lined with white satin; on his head was a richly jewelled cap of crimson velvet, of immense value, and round his neck he wore a collar studded with many precious

stones, of which I never saw the like.' At the instant he saw
the group, the king moved towards them, giving them his
hand to kiss; after which he 'embraced them with the greatest
possible demonstration of love and good will towards the most
illustrious Signory'.[28]

Royal conduct

Much was written about the conduct of inferiors to their
lords and masters, but the exact behaviour between the heads
of states was less often recorded. State etiquette at the courts
of England and France was very similar, because the English,
nobility for many years borrowed largely from the manners
of the French. Therefore, the account of the meeting between
Louis XII of France, and Philip, Archduke of Austria, would be
representative of the conduct between royal persons on state
occasions. The hall where the French king waited was richly
hung with cloth of gold, and was so crammed with people
that it was not easy to enter. At the entrance, the archduke
removed his cap, whereupon he was announced to the king:
'Sire, voila Monsieur l'Archduke!' to which the king smilingly
replied: 'Voila un beau Prince.' The archduke then made his
first bow, just inside the doorway, and the king rose up from
his seat, beginning to walk slowly towards his guest. As the
archduke made his second bow, near the centre of the hall,
the king removed his own cap; the third obeisance was made
near the king, who then embraced the archduke, speaking
courteously to him in an undertone. King Louis then replaced
his own cap, pressing the duke to do the same, but Philip
insisted that it was his 'duty' towards the king to remain uncovered.

Not all countries of Europe used the same forms of etiquette, particularly where the kiss of greeting between the
sexes was observed. The custom of Spain differed from that
of most northern countries, including England. When the turn
came for Joanna (named the Mad) to be presented to Louis
XII of France after her husband the archduke, she was asked
whether or not she would use the kiss of greeting to his

[28] Rawden Brown (Trans. and Ed.): *Four years at the court of Henry
VIII. A Selection of Dispatches written by Sebastian Giustinian*. London,
1854. Vol. 1, pp. 72 and 78.

Majesty. Advised by the Bishop of Cordova, she said she would use this ceremony. The French king advanced to greet her without delay, so that she had barely time to make her two deep curtsies before he raised her to embrace her, his cap in his hand. Then, taking her by the arm and placing her 'above' him (this usually meant the right-hand side), he led her through the hall to the chair placed for her.[29]

[29] T. Godefroy: *Le Cérémonial Français*. Paris, 1649.

CHAPTER III

Elizabethan

(a) DEPORTMENT AND ETIQUETTE

The courts of kings and princes remained the heart of the polite world. To these centres men looked for guidance in the refinement of manners and the social graces.

> *Of Court it seems, men Courtesie do call,*
> *For that it there most useth to abound,*
> *And well beseemeth that in Princes hall,*
> *That vertue should be plentifully found,*
> *Which of all goodly manner is the ground,*
>   *And roote of civill conversation.*
>   Edmund Spenser[1]

The old idea that the nobility should set an example of good manners continued to be taught and was upheld by the schoolmaster, Roger Ascham: 'Great men in Court, by their example, make or marre all other men's manners. Take heed therefore, ye great ones in ye Court, yea, though ye be ye greatest of all, take heed what ye do, take heed how ye live. For as you great ones use to do, so all mean men love to do. You be indeed, makers or marrers of all men's manners within the Realm.' The English court, said Ascham, could profit by studying *Il Cortegiano* (*The Book of the Courtier*) without slavishly copying Italian fashions. The English were apt to imitate the foolish, unworthy behaviour 'which you gather in Italy', by 'fond books, of late translated out of Italian into English, sold in every shop in London'.[2] The whole of Europe was indebted to Italy for the example she set in politer living

---

1 Edmund Spenser: from *England's Parnassus*. London, 1600.
2 Roger Ascham: *The Schoolmaster*. London, 1570.

and refinement of manners. Her influence in all spheres of life was felt particularly in the arts of bodily exercise; in riding, fencing, and dancing instruction she led the world. In the last named was included the behaviour and manners of good society. Each country translated these ideas to suit their temperament. 'Heare,' cried Ascham, 'what the Italian sayeth of the English man: . . . *"Englese Italiano, e un diablo incarnato!"* ' But the poet, Robert Greene, denying this, wrote, 'only I am English born, and I have English thoughts, not a devil incarnate because I am Italianate'. Since the common people of England would be little affected by the ever-changing courtly fashions, Touchstone's gibe rings true, that no man who had not been at Court could know 'good behaviour' – this being distinct from 'good manners'.

The apparent desire among the English for copying foreign fashions was the constant theme of critics of contemporary behaviour from the sixteenth to the eighteenth century. In the seventeenth and eighteenth centuries, the rage was for French fashions and behaviour; in the sixteenth, Italian and Spanish vied with French. A fanciful discourse of the subject between a country gentleman and a courtier (1586), puts the gentleman's view that it was 'a strange matter to see how men in this age, and in this realm of England, begin to alter their manners and customs, not only in garments and ordinary behaviour (which be things of more importance), but even in their order of life and conversation. . . . Indeed, I am a home bred bird, and therefore will not take upon me to discourse of foreign customs . . . but, as I told you at the first, I am sorry to see the English men so apt to leave their ancient, good fashions, and fall into foreign manners'. The courtier does not wholly agree – 'it is true that some men do, but the most do not' – and in reply to the gentleman's dislike of 'superfluous ceremony' retorts that the latter uses 'more ceremony than I, that have spent some part of my life in countries where those customs are most plentiful.'[3]

ELIZABETHAN MAN

Rules of polite behaviour, arising in the long-forgotten past

[3] Nicholas Breton: *The English Courtier and the Country Gentleman.* 1586. London, 1868.

from the dictates of tribal law, had been regulated throughout the Middle Ages mostly by traditional precepts of precedence. But in the late sixteenth century they began to be regarded in a different, more personal light. The stamp of approval was accorded to courtesy in its own right, and although precedence played a major role still in the courtly etiquette of the day, it was no longer the only criterion of merit or consideration.

'The Courtier ought to accompany all his doings, gestures, demeanours: finally his motions with a grace,' wrote Castiglione, 'And this, me thinke, ye put for a sauce to everie thing, without the which all his other properties and good conditions were little worth.' Such sentiments, reminiscent of Cicero, echo again and again through the ages. Not all the people of different nations, however, are moulded in one form. Movement acquires a national characteristic as do other forms of outward expression. Castiglione, for example, found 'the peculiar quiet gravitie of the Spaniardes' more agreeable to his Italian nature than that of the French, whose 'quick liveninesse . . . is perceived . . . almost in everie gesture'.[4] He disapproved of his countrymen affecting to copy French manners – nodding and shaking their heads and so forth.

A work published in 1581 takes another view of Italian mannerisms. 'The fashion of the natives or people of the East, the outward gestures and customs received among them [are] contrary . . . to the Western people. . . . Those which draw nigh unto the East and South are, by reason of the heat, more easie to move themselves, and consequently to make and show gestures. Northerners, by reason of the cold be more heavy and weighty. . . . The Italian in his . . . speeche . . . intermingleth and useth so many gestures, that if an Englishman should see him afar off, not hearing his words, would judge him out of his wit, or else playing some comedy upon a scaffold.' In comparison, the anonymous writer continues, a German preaching from the pulpit would appear as though unable to use his limbs.[5]

The importance of knowing one's place in the hierarchy of the aristocracy was instilled from an early age. It is almost

[4] Castiglione: *The Book of the Courtier.* Everyman. London, 1928. p. 43.
[5] Anon: *A Treatise of Daunces.* London, 1581.

true that every action was conditioned by rules of precedence. Not only did men have to observe due respect towards their superiors, but they themselves must not allow any disrespect of their own status to pass unnoticed. Should the host at a dinner 'be so gross and careless' as to place a man at table in a lower place than his due, it would not be correct for the guest to dispute the point; nevertheless, it was in order that a young man, finding himself in this situation, 'should be furnished with some girding speeches', to let his host and the other guests know that his acceptance was not due to his ignorance of the correct rules.[6]

It was expected, however, that the courteous gentleman would show consideration for others in his behaviour, observing the small courtesies like any man or woman of good manners. If, for example, at a ball, a gentleman sat down on a seat just vacated by another, it was good manners to give it up, or at least to rise, when the previous occupant returned. This, so he was told, would cause him to be praised and admired by all – apart from his having done an act worthy of a well-mannered gentleman. What is more, he would have averted a possible quarrel, much to the relief of the company.

How to sit

When in company, the gentleman had to remember not only whether he occupied the correct seat, but also to occupy it with grace, especially when circumstances rendered him in any way conspicuous. Grace was now regarded as essential to the polished gentleman, so by sitting in an ungainly fashion he made himself 'an ugly and disorderly sight to the beholders'. He was advised to sit not too far back in his chair, which enabled him to place both feet on the ground 'almost side by side, not crossed or wide apart as some are wont to have them', but with ease and 'all decorum'.

The elegant posture to adopt, if seated in a chair with arms, was to rest the left arm along the chair-arm, while the right, resting on the elbow, held in the hand such trifles as 'a handkerchief, gloves or a flower, to give himself grace'.

[6] Anon: *The Court of Civill Courtesie*. London, 1591.

The Hat

The hat, or cap, was never removed unless in salutation, or in deference to those of superior degree. To wear it pulled over the eyes, or on one side, was contrary to elegance.

The Rapier

Rapiers with beautifully fashioned hilts and Toledo blades gave a decorative appearance to their wearers, who would never have been seen in public without them at their sides, even when at a ball. When dancing galliards and other lively dances, it was in order for gallants to lay aside their rapiers and their cloaks or capes. The exception, it seems, was Italy where the gentlemen were told how to manipulate rapiers so that these were never impeded by the cloak, otherwise a man's life might be endangered in a sudden quarrel. The length of the rapier made it a somewhat awkward instrument to control, particularly in a crowd. If, when seated, the point protruded behind the chair, it could cause someone passing behind to stumble inadvertently, which might result in a fight. On going to sit down, 'it is your duty', says the book of manners, 'to give a slight bow to those who are near', then with the cap in the right hand, 'with your left you will put your sword [point] forward, and sit down with every grace on your chair or bench; when settled, you will put on your gloves if you think fit'.[7]

When moving in a crowd, or dancing in column formation with another couple close behind, or in 'figured' dances, the hilt of the rapier was lifted so that the point hung perpendicularly beside the left leg. Men who adopted a swaggering posture, with the hilt pressed downwards by the left hand, were likened to the character of 'a captain in a Spanish comedy'.

Gloves

Gloves could be rather a trial, for they were continually having to be taken off and put on again. At this period it was

[7] F. Caroso: *Della Nobiltà di Dame*. Venice, 1600. There is no published translation of the whole of this book. The section on deportment, from which these quotations are taken, has been translated for the author by the late Miss Alison Brothers.

considered bad manners, and even ridiculous, to offer a gloved hand to a lady whether leading her in a dance or on other occasions of etiquette. Similarly, ladies who did not remove their gloves when taking a gentleman's hand were 'laughed at and derided by all', so that it was hardly fair to accuse them, as one writer did, of continually pulling off and putting on their gloves.

Gloves and gauntlets could be very ornamental, of fine Spanish leather, embroidered and fringed and possibly scented, even for men. The fashion at this period was to wear them tight-fitting, with the heavy jewelled rings outside the gloved fingers. This tightness could cause moments of embarrassment. Some gentlemen wore gloves so fashionably tight that, when invited to take a lady's hand (as occurred where there was dancing) they took 'more than the space of an *Ave Maria* to get them off', thus keeping the lady waiting, who was obliged to hide her smiles behind her fan. Some, by using their teeth to assist them were left with one finger of the glove in the mouth, 'upon which all fell to laughing'.

Walking

Della Casa, in his pertinent observations on men and manners, did not spare those who moved with an ill grace, or in an affected fashion. Some flung their arms about so that onlookers would think that they 'were sowing corn in a field'. Others made almost as much noise as a cart by stamping their pattened feet on the street cobbles – though it was not seemly that men should walk 'so soft and demurely as a maid'. Some, like country louts, went about staring others in the face, or walked splay-footed, or fidgeted a-quivering with their legs as they stood to talk with a friend. Others, thinking too much of their appearance, kept stooping to 'stroke up their hose' or, in the belief that they cut a fine, military figure, with a hand on the hip, appeared to 'jet up and down like a peacock' as they walked.[8]

The manner in which people walk is affected by their footwear. In our own times women walk differently according to whether they wear low- or high-heeled shoes. Fashion pays

[8] Giovanni Della Casa: *Galateo*. London, 1576.

little heed to comfort, and is a truly difficult force to with-stand. This strange force of public opinion has caused people of all nations and all periods to torture their bodies and their feet in order to be fashionable.

For indoor wear, men and women of the sixteenth century had close-fitting, heel-less shoes made of satin, velvet, silk, cloth, or leather. Out of doors these 'pumps' were protected from the mud and wet by pattens or by overshoes named pantofles (in Italian, *pianelle*), thus forming 'double-soled' shoes (Plates VIIIc, Xa and c, XVIc and e). One of the duties of a page was to carry his master's pantofles, as at a ball, when his master discarded these to trip 'light-footed'. In the early seventeenth century, dancing-schools seemed 'to be places consecrated; for they that use to practise here put off their shoes and dance *single-soled*'. Instructions given to dancers confirm that the overshoe was removed for dancing, at least by men, who were not supposed to dance wearing *pianelle*. Women, whose steps, though nimble, were not as energetic as those of men, were advised to learn how to manage their *pianelle*, to prevent them falling off their feet.

These pantofles, worn from the close of Elizabeth's reign up to the eighteenth century, were intended as fashionable foot-wear for indoors, being made of rich materials – leather or velvet, coloured black, white, red or green, and decorated with gold or silver thread or silk. In time, these fancy pantofles were used out of doors, in place of the more serviceable 'pattens' made of wood. 'To what good uses serve these Pant-offles,' asks Stubbs, 'except it be to wear in a private house, or in a man's chamber to keep him warm (for this is the only use whereto they best serve in my judgment); but to go abroad in them as they are now used . . . is rather . . . a hindrance . . . than otherwise', it being necessary 'to knock and spurne at every wall, stone or post to keep them on.' How, he asks, could these pantofles be thought an advantage when the wearer could not walk steadily in them 'without slipping and sliding at every pace'; and how could they be described as elegant when, with their 'flipping and flapping up and down in the dirt' such a heap of mire collected on them that the wearer was loaded with an importable burden'.[9] Moreover, the heel some-

[9] Philip Stubbs: *The Anatomie of Abuses*. London, 1583.

times hung an inch or two over the end of the pantofle, causing in some cases swelling of the legs.

In the following century Samuel Pepys, taking his wife to dine with Mr Pierce, found that she was 'exceedingly troubled with a pair of new pattens, and I vexed to go so slow, it being late'. In such foot-wear progress could not have been hurried, although in normal circumstances people did not entertain the notion of hurrying. Their lives were not ruled by the ruthless mechanism of a timepiece. 'I would not have a gentleman to run in the street, nor go too fast', says Della Casa, an observation which was still being repeated in the nineteenth century. Haste was deemed right only for lackeys and servants. For a gentleman to sweat and puff, or tire himself, did not conform to the notion of dignity on which they modelled their behaviour.

Fashionable airs

Men allow fashion to make fools of them, not only in their dress, but in their manners also, by following too apishly every passing trend of the day. The sixteenth century was the Age of the Courtier *par excellence*. This entailed tedious hours of hanging around the courts of royal or noble establishments; hours which were spent in gaming, gossip, and the invention of fanciful airs and graces, always associated with courtiers of lesser calibre than those who were not tempted by such trifles.

Men of perception, in all ages, have been amused, bored, or disgusted by such vanities, which nevertheless often provided authors and playwrights with rich material. Castiglione poked fun at the courtier who carried his head so carefully for fear of ruffling his hair; who kept 'in the bottom of his cap a looking glass and a comb in his sleeve', and who had a page with a sponge and brush in constant attendance. But such a man appears on the stage in *Cynthia's Revels*[10]: 'Where is your page? call for your casting bottle,[11] and place your mirror in

---

[10] Ben Jonson: *Cynthia's Revels*. Act II i. Everyman, Dent, 1934.

[11] 'An excellent sweet water for a casting bottle: Take three drams of oyle of Spike, one dramme of oyle of Thyme, one dramme of oyle of Lemons, one dramme of oyle of Cloves . . . one graine of Civet [and a little of a mixture previously described]. . . .Temper them well in a silver spoone with your finger . . . [gradually wash out the oil from the spoon into a "silver ball" or bowl].' Platt: *Delightes for Ladies to adorn their persons*. London, 1609.

your hat, as I told you: so!' This play, dedicated to 'The Special fountain of manners – The Court', is loaded with allusions to the affectations of courtiers – a valuable sidelight on their strange and restricted world. The courtier 'made all of clothes and face', mincing his way through life; his actions, expressions, and speech all set, as though rehearsed. His piece done, he –

> Then walks off melancholic, and stands wreath'd
> As he were pinn'd up to the arras, thus.[12]

'Why', asks Tommaso Buoni, 'doth the sweetness of speech and comely carriage of the body give greater grace unto Beauty than any other part?' Perhaps, he muses, because beauty 'without that grace . . . either in the tongue or in the motion of the body, seemeth the Beauty of an Image, drawn in dead colours'. The young think more of beauty of body; the old of beauty of mind; whereas with princes and women of honourable birth 'we do not admire so much the singular Beauty of their bodies, as their gracious carriage, their sweet speech . . .' All men 'endeavour by art to seem that they are not. And for this cause proceedeth their exquisiteness, their art . . . their care in their apparel, their Gate, their speech'. To the eyes of the world, especially to their lovers, they wish to present a 'comely carriage'. Their material wealth was to be seen 'by their rich apparel; their Rings, their Diamonds, their Rubies, their Chaines, their Gold; their horses, their servants; their multitude of friends, their liberality'. Wealth was to be displayed upon the person, and in possessions. Only the eccentric would hoard their riches while appearing in slovenly attire.[13]

Grace of speech and demeanour, if not inborn or acquired through education, could never be assumed or discarded at will like a garment. Cleland, writing in 1607, likened it to a garment fashioned by the mind: "To conclude this general behaviour, me-thinks it is a fit and well made garment of the mind, and should have the conditions of a garment, *viz*, that it be made in fashion; that it be not too curious, but shaped

---

[12] *Cynthia's Revels*, Act III. ii.
[13] Tommaso Buoni: *Problems of Beautie and all humane affections.* Trans. Lennard. London, 1606.

so that it may set forth any good making of the mind, and hide any deformity.'[14]

Those who imagined they could add to their stature by assuming an air of importance drew nothing but ridicule upon themselves. Some men, of no great worth, said Della Casa, were so pompous, using 'such a solemnity in all their doings', walking 'so stately', speaking as if they sat in the seat of judgement that it was 'a very death to behold them'. The man of worth, the true 'gentle man' on the other hand, steps forth from Edmund Spenser's Gentlenesse:

> The gentle mind by gentle deeds is knowne.
> For a man by nothing is so well bewrayd,
> As by his manners, in which plaine is showne
> Of what degree and what race he is growne.
> Faerie Queene, VI. c. iii. i.

Pomanders, fans, tobacco

Pomanders (Plate XVIa) were used by both men and women – 'I'll have your chain of pomander, sirrah; what's your price?' says Mercury in Cynthia's Revels. So too were fans before they became the monopoly of women, for in the east, where they had originated, the possession of a fan was associated from time immemorial with persons of the ruling class. It was not merely an attribute of femininity.

The taking of snuff and the inhaling of tobacco was 'greatlie taken up and used in England'. At various places of amusement – the theatre, bear- and bull-baiting, cock-fighting – the air was thick with tobacco smoke. 'By God's deins, I marle what pleasure or felicity they have in taking this roguish tobacco', says Cob in Every Man in his Humour, in 1598; 'it's good for nothing but to choke a man, and fill him full of smoke and embers.'[15] This was the opinion held by King James I who wrote Counterblast to Tobacco in 1604: '. . . is it not both great vanity and uncleanness, that at the table, a place of respect, of cleanliness, of modesty, men should not be ashamed to sit tossing of tobacco pipes . . . making the filthy smoke and stink thereof to exhale athwart the dishes, and infect

---

[14] Cleland: Hero-paideia. London, 1607.
[15] Jonson: Every Man in his Humour. Act III. ii., from Complete Plays of Ben Jonson. Vol. I. Everyman. Dent, 1934.

the air, when very often men that abhor it are at their
repast? ...'[16]

ELIZABETHAN WOMAN

The medieval lady was taught to observe a quiet, meek
demeanour, but her descendant of the later sixteenth century
was instructed more specifically. However fashionable and
carefully chosen were their clothes, young women were reminded that they achieved nothing if they did not know how
to behave. Many women, it was pointed out, 'either through
ignorance, want of instruction, or through affectation', spoiled
their appearances with silly gestures and foolish airs. Some
affected mannerisms as they walked along the streets; putting
on 'a little mumping mouth', and tripping along as though they
were about to dance. Others walked extremely slowly with
exaggerated care, or held themselves 'upright and stiff as an
Image'. Yet others were slatternly in their appearance, with
untidy hair falling around their necks, or hanging down their
backs – 'affecting carelessness'. On raising their skirts off the
ground, they revealed 'stained, wrinkled stockings and . . .
ridiculous shoes'. At all times young women had to behave
with discretion, avoiding foolish mannerisms which drew
remarks from onlookers, such as keeping their eyes always on
their feet, or upwards like 'star gazers', or 'catching flies' with
their mouths open.[17]

'I tell you,' said Caroso, 'that it is necessary for ladies to
learn the fair and honourable manners and ceremonies before
all else, particularly Noble and Very Noble Ladies; the reason
is that if they do not know what to do, persons who behold
them will say,"That Lady is too grand and puts on airs"; they
will not understand that it is only because she does not know
how to behave.'[18]

He begins his instructions by explaining how to make a
curtsy correctly. This learned, the lady proceeded to the proper
manner of walking, and of managing her *pianelle*.

According to Stubbs, women's 'corked shoes' (the thick soles
often being of cork), were similar in materials, colour, and

[16] King James I: *Counterblast to Tobacco*. London, 1604.
[17] Anon: *The Ladies Behaviour*, c. 1540. London, 1693.
[18] Caroso: *Della Nobiltà di Dame*. Venice, 1600.

embroidery to those worn by men. High chopines (*cioppinos*) (Plate XVI*f*), said Nicolo de Favri, were not worn as much in England as in Spain, Italy and France, but the fashion was not unknown here.

When the little Princess Henrietta Maria of France came to be the bride of King Charles I, she answered his remark about her height by saying that it was her true height, without the aid of artificial means. Very high chopines were much favoured by the aristocratic ladies of Venice. In the late fifteenth century these ladies were said to wear 'shoes called pianelle' so high that they were obliged to have attendants on whom they could lean lest they fell as they walked. During his visit to Venice in 1645, John Evelyn saw noblemen out walking with their ladies whose chopines were so high that they raised the wearers above everyone else as if on stilts. For support the proud ladies were forced to 'set their hands on the heads of two matron-like servants, or old women', who mumbled their beads as they went. Getting in and out of gondolas, of course, proved somewhat hazardous and a sight for ridicule.

The contemporary English stage was quick to satirize such a fashion. Ben Jonson's lady from Spain 'O, me, the very infanta of the giants!' is asked:

'And do they wear Cioppinos all? . . . I should think it hard to go in them, madam.

'At the first it is, madam.

'Do you never fall in them?

'Never.

'I swear I should, six times an hour.'[19]

Walking

Nevertheless, Caroso points out, the problem of how to 'keep one's *pianelle* properly on one's feet so that one does not sprain an ankle or become a mockery or drop them,' was very real. Some lords and ladies dragged their *pianelle* as they walked, making an unpleasant noise – a familiar enough sound in people's ears, for the clattering of wooden pattens must have been a common background noise to daily life.

The manner of walking suggested by Caroso was to raise

[19] Jonson: *The Devil is an Ass.* Act IV. i. Vol. II. Everyman. 1934.

first the toe of the moving foot, straightening the knee, so that even though the toe of the *pianelle* was lifted as much as 'a palm and a half' off the ground, the impression made on the onlooker would be that the foot was raised a mere three fingers in the air; then, by placing the foot down firmly, the lady would seem to walk 'with all grace, decorum and beauty'.

The Farthingale

The voluminous folds of a medieval lady's gown, from considerations of modesty, decorum, and convenience to all, had to be gathered around her, so that when walking the lady was never free from their weight upon her arms or hands. In the sixteenth century the introduction of the farthingale removed this burden, holding the skirts of the gown away from the feet in front, so that they lightly skimmed the ground. The consequent effect on women's deportment was considerable, even if, at the same time, the farthingale introduced new problems for them.

What is known as the 'Spanish' farthingale was favoured in Spain and Italy more than the so-called 'French' farthingale preferred in France, the Netherlands, and England. The second version cannot be described as an elegant garment, making the wearer appear very large round the waist. A small bolster rested on the hips, tied in front beneath the gown; or a frame in the shape of a wheel was made to stick out around the lady's waist, so that the gown spread over it (Plate XIIIa).

The Spanish farthingale was in the form of an under-petticoat, or possibly a frame held by cords, small at the waist and increasing in circumference towards the hem by hoops of widening diameter. It was worn over the under-robe, and extended the skirts of the upper gown to give a bell-like shape. This is much the most becoming of the various kinds and can lend an air of elegance to the wearer if worn with care. To appear graceful when moving in this cage-like garment, it is essential to walk *smoothly*, otherwise the bobbing and swaying skirts can create an ugly effect. Walking smoothly, with rather short steps, the lady can appear to glide along, for the feet are not seen; a very slightly, rhythmical sway of the skirts may give an intriguing grace of movement, which is spoiled if exaggerated.

Sitting

When moving through a restricted space, also when sitting down, the farthingale required some care in its management, though we learn from Caroso that this care was frequently lacking. 'Women', he says, 'generally sit down carelessly, without any manners or ceremony, and the train of their gowns remains outside the chair', thus getting in the way of those who wish to pass by. To remedy this, these ladies attempt 'to draw the train nearer with their foot'. Such an action, he remarks, 'Speaking freely, is just what cats do with their tails'. Nor was it an improvement, according to him, to lift the gown with the right hand, pulling it under the chair, particularly as some, in doing this, raised the farthingale 'as high as the belt'. In Caroso's opinion, women did this 'out of pride to show the beholders how beautiful are their petticoats'. Similarly, at balls or other places where the throng was great, ladies found it difficult to pass through the crowd to their seats without lifting their farthingales high in the air, over the heads of the seated guests. This was commonly regarded as most unbecoming behaviour. It could be avoided if other women gave way so that those passing might do so with the minimum lifting of the gown and a graceful bending of the body.

When sitting down, the train of the gown was to be adjusted as far as possible, not by the hand, but with the body and the aid of the farthingale. Approaching the chair, the lady turns slightly – 'with the person peacocking somewhat' – using her farthingale to put her train between the legs of the chair; . . . she must sit down half way up the seat for, if she were to seat herself too far back, the farthingale would so raise the gown in front that the persons facing her could see half way up her legs. But if . . . she sits down in the middle of the seat, her feet will rest together on the ground, and her farthingale and gown likewise'. She was never supposed to show her feet when seated (Plate XIa). 'Those poor ladies,' continues Caroso, 'whose gown rises up . . . strike at it with both hands; . . . they cannot make it go down because of the cords of the farthingale', and merely look 'as though they were trying to get rid of dust or fleas.'[20]

The correct posture when seated in polite company resembled that of the gentleman; the left arm fully extended along the arm of the chair; the right resting on the elbow, with the hand in her lap, or employed in holding a handkerchief, or a fan in warm weather and a muff in winter time. If seated upon a low chair without arms, or on a stool, she was to place her hands in her lap, the left being below the right; here also she was to be careful that the hem of her gown rested level on the ground. In order to appear self-assured and fully at ease, say Caroso, she must 'take care not to sit like a statue, but from time to time make some movement, or put on her gloves. If it is summer, she will fan herself gracefully with her fan, or try to hold some converse with the ladies among whom she is sitting, but above all, with modest eyes, not letting them stray now here, now there', since this would cause her to be judged vain and of little worth.[20]

Trinkets

In the fifteenth and sixteenth centuries an assortment of small objects was attached to the end of the lady's girdle-chain (Plate XVId). 'Give me my girdle and see that all the furniture be at it', is the command given to her maid by a lady at her toilet. Items she might require were her 'Cizers', pincers, pen-knife, 'the knife to close Letters', a bodkin, a case with an ear-picker, her seal, and a pomander. In addition she wore a purse on her gown, and the maid was to see that the silver 'Comfet box' was filled with comfets. Then she requested a clean handkerchief and some gloves, with a mask to wear when going out of doors, and a fan.[21]

Pomanders used in the fifteenth and sixteenth centuries were fairly heavy, made often of metal, beautifully worked, in size somewhat larger than a golf ball. They contained separately hinged partitions, held together by a central pin with a screw at the top (Plate XVIa). The partitions shaped like the segments of an orange could contain different scents – musk, civet, and ambergris were favoured. Amongst recipes for making 'Sweete

[20] Caroso, op. cit.
[21] Peter Erondell: *The French Garden.* London, 1605.

and delicate Pomanders', is one of thrift: 'To renew the scent
of a Pomander, take one graine of civet (double the proportion
it will bee so much sweeter); grind them up on a stone with a
little Rosewater, and after wetting your hands with Rosewater,
you may work the same in[to] your Pomander. This is a sleight
to passe awaie an old Pomander, but my intention is honest.'[22]

In all, then, the lady carried a fair weight on her person,
and found it easier to draw up the length of chain into her
hand, to prevent its swinging and bumping against the legs
while walking or when dancing.

Fans

Fans, an importation from the east, did not become a regular
accessory of feminine attire until the second half of the sixteenth century. At this period fans were round in shape, and
mounted on a stick. It is the only period when the fan was
attached to the person, being hung by a ribbon or cord from
the waist. The folding fan, always carried in the hand, did not
become fashionable in England until the seventeenth century.

A gentlewoman of rank, who set out on horseback, required
six or eight serving-men to attend her. 'She must have one
to carry her Cloak and Hood lest it rain; another her Fan,
if she use it not herself; another her Box with Ruffs and other
necessaries; another behind whom her Maid or Gentlewoman
must ride; and some must be loose, to open Gates and supply
other services that may be occasioned.' So argued a member
of 'the gentlemanly profession of serving-men', who deplored
the current fashion of reducing expenditure by reducing the
numbers of servants in a nobleman's household. He admitted,
however, that 'a new invention', that of the wheeled vehicle,
made the number of attendants unnecessary now that ladies
of means had their own coaches 'wherein she, with her Gentlewoman, Maid and Children, and what necessaries . . . any of
them . . . use', could be carried 'with smaller charge'. All that
was required were 'one or two men, at the most, besides the
Coachman', these being quite sufficient 'for a Gentlewoman or
lady of worthy parentage'.[23]

[22] Platt: *Delightes for Ladies to adorn their persons.* London, 1609.
[23] Anon: *A Health to the Gentlemanly Profession of Servingmen.* London,
1598.

Courtly fashions

The fashion of carrying in the hand a handkerchief made of rich material, sometimes fringed and embroidered, is said to have been introduced from Italy, as were many other courtly fashions in this period. When dancing, ladies placed these showy handkerchiefs half in and half out of their wide sleeves 'for greater elegance'. In doing so, says Caroso, they should be careful to place it so that it would not drop out, as this caused various gentlemen present to run and pick it up. – 'like a flock of starlings, only to please the lady, so causing a disturbance'. Any small thing thus returned either to a lady, or even to a courtier of high degree, was accompanied by a courteous gesture of kissing the giver's own hand after the object had been presented. It might be that the giver pretended instead to kiss the object he was returning, and these courtesies were always accompanied with low bows: 'If I did but let my glove fall by chance, . . .' brags Robert Burton's amorous lady in *The Anatomy of Melancholy*, 'I had one of my suitors, nay, two or three at once, ready to stoop and take it up, and kiss it, and with a low congee deliver it unto me.'[24]

Visitors to this country appear to have been attracted by the natural beauty of English women. Samuel Keichel, a merchant from the duchy of Swabia, who was here about 1585, thought the women of England charming and very pretty. 'They do not falsify, paint or bedaub themselves as in Italy or other places', but he was not much taken with their style of dress.[25] Thomas Platter, in England in 1599, says much the same about the appearance of the women, who had 'mostly blue-grey eyes and are fair and pretty'. The burgher women, he says, wore 'high hats covered with velvet or silk', and instead of stiffening their bodices with whalebone, they wore 'a broad circular piece of wood over the breast to keep the body straighter and more erect'; noble ladies, on the other hand, copied French fashions.[26]

[24] Robert Burton: *The Anatomy of Melancholy*. Vol. III, Everyman. London, 1949. p. 161.
[25] W. Brenchley Rye: *England as seen by foreigners in the days of Elizabeth and James*. London, 1865.
[26] C. Williams (trans.): *Thomas Platter: Travels in England*. London, 1937.

The artificial painting of the face was remarked on by writers of this period including Castiglione speaking of his own country-women. It was understandable, he says, that women desired to appear beautiful, and that if they were not so by nature, they endeavoured to remedy this by art, by painting their faces and plucking their eyebrows and forehead – all those things 'that you women believe are kept very secret from men, and yet doe all men know them. . . . Doe you not marke how much more grace is in a woman, that if she does trimme her selfe, doth it so scarcely and so little that who so beholdeth her, standeth in doubt whether she bee trimmed or no; than in an other so bedawbed that a man would ween she had a viser on her face, and dareth not laugh for making it chappe.' Such a woman, having dressed in the morning so that she was encased in the rigid fashions of the age, appeared thereafter 'like an image of wood without moving'.

Qualities of feminine character were not very different from those of men, but goodness, courage, and wisdom alone were not sufficient for the lady whose sphere was within the arti-ficialities and pitfalls of court life. The good housewife, tending her husband's household and her children, would scarcely be an ornament at the table or entertainments provided by her husband's hospitality. The lady who would grace the house-hold of 'the perfect courtier', said Castiglione, 'belongeth unto her above all others thinges, a certaine sweetenesse in language that may delite whereby she may gently entertain all kinde of men with talke worthie the hearing and honest, and applyed to the time and place, and to the degree of the person she comuneth withal', accompanying all 'with sober and quiet manners . . . a readie livlinesse of wit, wherby she may declare her selfe far wide from all dulness'.[27]

(b) SALUTATIONS

Conventions of behaviour change less rapidly than do fashions in dress and similar modish fancies, so that, in the 'new world' of the first Elizabethans, the basic form of the old-world courtesy remained. In the everyday greeting of the

[27] Castiglione: *The Book of the Courtier*. Everyman. London, 1928.

bow, men continued to make 'curtseys' by bending their knees, but even this simple act reflected the contemporary interest in refinement of manners which was so marked a feature of this age. At the glittering courts of wealthy and powerful princes and lords, men and women now took such delight in analysing the attributes of elegant appearance and behaviour, that this furnished topics of 'sweete conversation' among courtiers assembled together for an evening's entertainment. No longer did the bow consist merely of genuflecting in reverential obeisance. The proper placing of the feet; the exact manner of drawing back the foot; the angle at which the knees were placed, or the body bowed, all could add to, or detract from, 'the handsomeness of person in making curtesie'.[28] Many scoffed at the new-fangled courtier, with his foreign 'cringes' and 'scrapings'; the direct simplicity of the medieval rever- ence now gave way to the studied grace of courtly artifice. At the same time humble country-folk (outside aristocratic circles) would be slow to alter their accustomed practice. '. . . those that are good manners at the court, are as ridiculous in the country as the behaviour of the country is most mockable at the court', is the reply of Shakespeare's simple Corin to Touch- stone's argument concerning manners in *As You Like It*.

Doffing the hat

We have shown it to have been the Italians who led the sixteenth century with books giving detailed instructions in manners. Caroso's 'Dialogue . . . on the Demeanour . . . of Gentlemen and Ladies', makes the doffing of the hat its 'First Rule', with the 'Second Rule' describing the bow. 'Among the actions which are of the greatest import – the doffing of the cap takes first place, as being the action devised by men to do honour and reverence to one another, even apart from the Dance.' He imparts his instruction in the form of a dialogue between the master and his pupil, a literary convention familiar at this period. The ancient theory of the superiority of the right over the left hand is introduced here again as an explan- ation of why men used the right hand to remove the hat from the head:

[28] 'O sweet Fastidious! O fine courtier!
How comely he bowes him in his court'sie!'
      Ben Jonson: *Every Man out of his Humour.*

Pupil: 'This doffing of the hat, or cap, what does it signify? And for what reason does one doff it with the right hand rather than the left?'

Master: 'Know, my son, that the doffing of the hat or cap, signifies no more than the honouring of the person whom one has a mind to honour; and the honour that one does is to uncover the worthiest and noblest part that a man has; and for this reason the hat must be doffed with the right hand, which is apter at learning to grasp things, besides being worthier and nobler than the left.'

The manner in which a man removed his hat in salutation became one of the indefinable adjuncts of well-bred behaviour. The method of lifting it off the head and holding it afterwards in the hand has varied according to the period and to the shape of the hat, but in every age there has been a right and a wrong way of doing this. 'Therefore,' says Caroso, 'to doff the cap and hold it in the hand in the most elegant and grace-ful way which can adorn any man, it is well to take the cap, or hat, by the band (if it be a cap), or the brim (if it be a hat) and lift it from the head, bringing the right arm well down. . . . One must keep the inside of the cap turned towards one's thigh after one has doffed it, and feign to kiss one's left hand; this being the heart hand, makes the action heartfelt.' It was wrong to clutch the cap with the 'whole hand' rather than with the

---

PLATE V

a. Men and women kneeling on both knees, in veneration of the Relics of St. Ursula. From the *St. Ursula Legend.* Convent of the Soeurs Noires, Bruges. Late fifteenth century.

b. English ambassadors received by the French King. *Froissart's Chronicles*, illustrated in the fifteenth century. (*Reproduced by courtesy of the Trustees of the British Museum.*)

c. Kneeling to hand a letter. Note chair of estate with canopy; windows glazed, with wooden shutters, and stone-flagged floor. Men wearing riding boots; the second man has thrown the chaperon scarf over his shoulder. *Roman de la Rose.* (*Reproduced by courtesy of the Trustees of the British Museum.*)

d. Roger d'Espaine and Espaing de Lyon welcomed at Toulouse. The man's bow combined with the hand-clasp. High hats and chaperons are worn. *Froissart.* (*Reproduced by courtesy of the Trustees of the British Museum.*)

b.

c.

d.

V. The man's reverence in Medieval times

a.

b.

c.

VI.   The lady's reverence, and deportment of ladies in sitting.
Furnishings, and the interiors of rooms

fingers. Also to hold it with the arm drawn back, the inside uppermost, looking like 'a poor wretch begging for alms'. Or to hold it so that the inside was visible for this revealed to 'the persons in front or behind, the grease which is wont to adhere to the brim, for one cannot always wear a new cap'. After doffing the cap, it was wrong to pretend to kiss it instead of one's hand.

The Bow

Having doffed the hat, the bow begins. Further theories concerning right and left-handedness enter into the discussion.

Pupil: Which foot must it be done with, the right or the left?

Master: I tell you that it must always be done with the left foot.

Pupil: Why with the left rather than with the right? For, a little while ago, Your Honour told me that in doffing the cap one must use the right hand since it is nobler than the left.

Master: These are the reasons why Reverence must be done with the left foot; first, because the right foot gives firmness and stability to the body; because of this the movement must be made with the left foot, which is the weaker; secondly one reveres the person to whom one is making the reverence from

---

PLATE VI

a. Two ladies about to kneel; people seated at ease, chins resting on their hands. Frontispiece to an early fifteenth-century edition of Chaucer's *Troylus and Cryseyde.* (*Reproduced by courtesy of The Master, Librarian and Fellows of Corpus Christi College, Cambridge.*)

b. Lady seated demurely, hands in her lap, while her companion uses gestures in conversation. Note wainscot seat and flagged floor. *Roman de la Rose.* (*Reproduced by courtesy of the Trustees of the British Museum.*)

c. Christine de Pisan kneeling as she offers her work to Isabella of Bavaria. Note deportment of seated ladies; and the bed with tester. The windows have glass and wooden shutters, and tapestries hang on the walls. *Christine de Pisan, Poèmes.* (*Reproduced by courtesy of the Trustees of the British Museum.*)

F

the heart; and, since the left foot is a member of the heart side, for this reason one must always use the left foot'[29] (Plate VIIIb).

'. . . let them curtsy with their left legs,' says Grumio in his order to the household servants, who also were to see '. . . their heads be slickly comb'd, their blue coats brush'd, and their garters of an indifferent knit' (The Taming of the Shrew, IV. i).

Following a salutation it was the accepted practice for a superior to request his inferior to replace his hat, and it was not out of place for the latter, in complying, to show some slight hesitancy in deference to his superior; but not on all occasions, nor at inappropriate times, as in Della Casa's example of a busy Judge who in saying 'Cover your head' meets with a man who, being 'so full of these ceremonies, after a number of legs[30] and shuffling curtsies, answers again "Sir I am very well thus". "But", says the Judge again, "Cover your head I say." Yet this good fellow, turning twice or thrice to and fro, making low congees down to the ground with much humility, answers him still, "I beseech your worship, let me do my duty".'[31]

The Curtsy

In the early sixteenth century the woman's mode of making a reverence was similar to the man's except that she kept her feet close together while bending the knees. As the lady's curtsy throughout the seventeenth and eighteenth centuries was made with the feet side by side, it is unlikely that a break in this tradition should occur for the second half of the sixteenth century. Unfortunately Arbeau is silent on this point, leaving the reader to draw his own conclusions from the small woodcut which shows the reverence (Plate VIIIa). Caroso's instructions, on the contrary, are given with his customary thoroughness and clarity.

On kissing the hand

In early times the gesture of 'adoration' whereby a wor-

[29] Caroso: Della Nobiltà di Dame. Venice, 1600.
[30] legs = bows.
[31] Della Casa: Galateo. London, 1576.

shipper carried his *own* hand to his mouth, kissing it 'to' the person or object of veneration, was associated with priests and religious ceremonial. Again, obsequious flattery paid to ancient god-kings and emperors made them the recipients of these forms of ceremony, and from this gradually followed the adoption of such customs within the circles of court life. 'Those solemnities that church men doe use at their Altars, and in their divine service bothe to God and his holy things, are properly called Ceremonies: but after, men did begin to reverence eche other with curious entertainements . . . amongst them selves, yealding, bending, and bowing their bodies, in token of reverence one to another, uncovering their heads, using highe titles and Styles of honour, and kissing their hands as if they were hollye things.' So wrote Della Casa, adding that these fashions were not of Italian origin, but were 'barbarous and straunge and not long since, from whence I knowe not, transported into Italie'. Other 'superstitious ceremonies' he believed 'were transported out of Spaine into Italie'.[32] It is certain that the Spanish court of this age was burdened with the most elaborate etiquette of any European nation, an etiquette which undoubtedly owed much to the Arab-Hebraic influence of many generations. Amongst peoples of the Near East, the hand-kiss gesture of salutation has been known since biblical times.

In England the practice drew satirical comment from contemporary playwrights, and appears to have been fashionable in court society for a period extending from the late sixteenth century to the Restoration. During this time the influence, first of the Italian Renaissance and then of the French court, was at its strongest. How much the ordinary English gentleman and lady, or even those attached to the court, made use of the fashion is not so easy to judge, and certainly the humble folk were unaccustomed to such tricks.

'*Corin:* . . . You told me you salute not at the court, but you kiss your hands; that courtesy would be uncleanly if courtiers were shepherds. *Touchstone:* Instance, briefly; come, instance. *Corin:* Why we are still handling our ewes; and their fells, you know, are greasy. . . . And they are often tarr'd over

[32] ibid.

with the surgery of our sheep; and would you have us kiss
tar?'[33]

Ordinary servants, likewise, would not use these affectations. The service they gave their masters was taken for granted,
being performed with simple courtesy. Says Della Casa:
'Neither must handicraft men, nor men of base condition, busy
themselves too much in over solemn ceremonies to great men,
and lords: it is not looked for in such. . . . And therefore it is
a foul fault in a servant to offer his master his service, for he
counts it his shame, and he thinks the servant doth make a
doubt whether he is master or no; as if it were not in him to
employ him, and command him too.'[34] Grumio's orders in *The
Taming of the Shrew*, IV, i, draw attention to this latest of
fashions: the servants must 'not presume to touch a hair of
my master's horsetail, till they kiss their hands'; a point better
understood by contemporary audiences than by those of
today.

Castiglione and Della Casa both condemn the tedious ceremony indulged in by some who, by word and gesture, over-
did the normal practices of courtesy, the 'sort of ceremonious
people who make it an art and merchandise, and keep a book
and a reckoning of it'.

The same opinion is expressed by Caroso himself. Despite
the fact that his book aims to teach these outward forms of
elegance, he tells his readers: 'Know then, that superfluous,
vain and exquisite ceremonies are ill-concealed flatteries, or
even manifest ones, known to all. So that, those who make a
great many *reverences*, dragging their feet, kissing their hands
and caps, and bowing and scraping to the ladies of their choice,
though they think to gain thereby can only lose; for their
fawning manners make them unpleasing and wearisome to the
said ladies. And those who attempt to act thus affectedly and
oddly, do it out of folly and vanity, like men of little worth,
as *Galateo* saith.'[35] True manners, the manners of the heart,
had little in common with the passing oddities of superficial
fancies. 'Truly, madam,' says Clown in *All's Well That Ends
Well*, 'If God have lent a man any manners, he may easily

[33] Shakespeare: *As You Like It.* III, ii.
[34] Della Casa: *Galateo.*
[35] Caroso: *Della Nobiltà di Dame.*

put it off at court. He that cannot make a leg, put off's cap, kiss his hand, and say nothing, has neither leg, hands, lip, nor cap; and indeed such a fellow, to say precisely, were not for the court: but, for me, I have an answer will serve all men.'[36]

But the heart alone does not teach the many little formalities with which men surround their social functions. Amongst courtiers of the Renaissance these were very precise.

Many references to the kissing of the hand occur throughout the plays of Ben Jonson but, again, it is from Caroso that we learn how this was done. It was always the right hand, which should not touch the mouth, being kept 'somewhat distant, and bending it a little, not keeping it straight', and the gesture was accompanied by either a bow or a curtsy. When raising the arm and bringing the hand towards the mouth, with the wrist and hand curving inwards, the index finger (often the favourite finger for a ring in these times) was nearest the mouth – 'with kissing your finger that hath the ruby' as Ben Johnson says. (Plates VIIIc and d, XVId.)

The custom, known from antiquity, of kissing the knee of great personages is mentioned by Caroso. At social functions where there were present those of royal or noble blood, a lady who greeted another, first kissing her own hand, made a slow reverence while 'pretending to kiss the princess's right hand'. But she must pretend to kiss her knee if the object of the salute was someone of greatly superior rank.

Likewise, when a prince or lord received the audience of the king in order to present a petition, in making a very low reverence before the king 'so that his knee almost touches the ground' he had to pretend to kiss the king's knee, 'and then, raising his face, he will kiss the petition and hand it to the king'. On taking his leave he went again through the motions of 'wishing to kiss his knee'.

In August 1564, the University of Cambridge received a visit from Queen Elizabeth. On entering Queens' College 'when Her Majesty was about the middle of the scholars, or sophisters, two – appointed for the same – came forth, and kneeled before her Grace and, kissing their papers, exhibited the same unto

[36] *All's Well That Ends Well.* II, ii.

her Majesty'. For the ceremony of delivering up the beadles' staffs on the same occasion, 'the bedells, kneeling, kissed their staves, and so delivered them to Mr Secretary, who likewise kissed the same, and delivered them to the Queen's hands, who could not well hold them. And her Grace gently and merrily re-delivered them, willing him and other magistrates of the University to minister justice uprightly, as she trusted they did.'[37]

(c) HOSTS AND GUESTS

Since Italy led Europe in matters of courtesy, Italian authors at this time were authorities on questions of etiquette. The influence of Castiglione's *The Courtier* was acknowledged in contemporary works concerned with courtly manners and occupations. The model of good behaviour laid down by Caroso was likely to be found in the polite circles of European society of the age. From Caroso we learn the etiquette of visiting, of behaviour towards royal and noble persons, and how people behaved at other social gatherings.

Visits
Courtesy visits were made for the purpose of offering congratulations, condolences, or merely to ensure that one's existence was not forgotten by those with whom it was expedient to remain in contact. Congratulations were tendered on the occasion of a wedding or a birth; condolences for illness or death. A young bride was taught the correct manner of greeting and entertaining all who honoured her by attending her nuptials. 'When a lady goes to a wedding feast' says Caroso, 'however great a lady she may be, she will go straight to the bride and, drawing near, make her a reverence, kissing her own right hand. At that instant, the bride and the other ladies who are seated at the said feast, will rise from their chairs and graciously kiss their own right hands, and gather together, doing the reverence. . . . When a duchess, or princess, appears in the room it is necessary for the bride to rise to her feet, with the other ladies who were seated and, with her mother, or sisters, or kinswomen, she will go to meet her.

[37] Francis Peck: *Desiderata Curiosa*. London, 1779.

And, when near to her they will make her a slow reverence, pretending to kiss their hands. Then, with her right hand, the bride will take the princess's left [thereby] giving her precedence, even if she tries not to accept it, and thus conduct her to a seat where she herself was sitting. Before sitting down, she must make another reverence, and the princess must return the honour before seating herself; also to those ladies who, by making the reverence together have done her honour. They will not sit down before the princess. Afterwards, with pleasant and delightful discourse, she will entertain the princess, as ladies are wont to do.'[38]

> Then fall they in discourse
> Of tires and fashions, how they must take place,
> Where they may kiss, and whom, when to sit down,
> And with what grace to rise; if they salute,
> What court'sy they must use; such cobweb stuff
> As would enforce the common'st sense abhor
> The'Arachnean workers.[39]

Thus are the court ladies pictured by Ben Jonson, weaving their interminable webs of flimsy nothingness.

The departure of the great lady necessitated similar ceremony. On rising from her seat, she curtsied to the bride and other ladies, who all rose and returned the curtsy. The bride, on rising from her deep curtsy, by a turn of her head, indicated to the company that she asked their pardon for being obliged to leave them in order to accompany her guest. Once again placing herself on the left-hand side, the bride led her visitor to the door, followed by her kinswomen. At the door, while making a deep curtsy, the bride kissed the lady's hand, thanking her for the great honour she had done in coming to the wedding ceremony. Returning to her seat, she curtsied again to the company, who had remained standing, whereupon, once more, they all sat down together. On the departure of any lady of less exalted rank, the bride merely rose to her feet, curtsied to her while kissing her own hand, and just touching the hand of her guest; 'Then she will sit down again, and so on, one after another'.

---

[38] Caroso: *Della Nobiltà di Dame*.
[39] Jonson: *Cynthia's Revels*. Act III. ii.

Balls and other festivities

As a rule, celebrations of most kinds were accompanied by dancing. In spite of the fact that at all such functions the proceedings were regulated by the rules of precedence, it seems that there were those who paid scant attention to precedence. Caroso says that even when dignitaries were present, as cardinals, dukes, princes, marquises, counts, lords, and knights who were 'entitled by precedence . . . to sit in their deputed places as the Order of Chivalry requireth', it had become the practice for those who arrived later 'to send for a chair, either high or low, and have it put in front of the Prince who was seated first'. And so they continued, each putting themselves before the others, of whatever rank. In time, everyone following this bad example, the space for dancing became restricted; moreover, since it was the etiquette at these balls, for the ladies to sit apart from the men, the encroachment thus made on the dancing space brought the chairs of the gentlemen and ladies nearer and nearer together. Since decorum did not approve this, also because of the clamour and disputes which arose, the hosts sometimes preferred to end the ball.

Much of the trouble was due to the fact that women, as well as men, invited their partners to dance. The men seated at the back were likely to miss the opportunity of being invited – the ladies often being somewhat timorous in the manner of making their invitation. On approaching, for example, the place where the men were seated, the ladies were apt to keep 'their eyes too low so that the cavaliers do not know which of them is being invited and the wrong ones rise. And sometimes, through their great desire to dance, the cavaliers hold out their hands to the lady, and she does not know which to take.' Other ladies often started a dispute, if it so happened that the wrong gentleman rose to dance, by saying that she did not invite him, but another; 'this is bad, for, since the cavalier has risen to his feet, the lady should dance with him for his honour's sake'.

It is wrong, also, for a lady to invite a man to dance 'with motions of the hand or head', or to call him by name. The invitation was to be made always with a curtsy. The lady should look directly at the cavalier, who thereupon would

rise to his feet, while she made him a curtsy. She then turned
a little sideways to him, pretending to 'arrange her dress, shifting it, and peacocking somewhat', to give him time to remove
his (probably) rather tight glove. For her to stand facing him
for this space of time was not considered proper – 'for it would
look as though they were making love'.

Many dances of this and later periods were performed by
a single couple while the rest of the company sat by and
watched, waiting for their own turn to dance. At times, if the
throng was great, it happened that they waited all evening
without dancing. 'Oft-times' Caroso remarked, 'it happens that
ladies go to Balls without ever being invited to dance. But
they ought not to be melancholy or sad, but force themselves
to seem as gay as they can by talking to the other ladies sitting
at their sides.' At least these ladies could comfort themselves
with the knowledge that it was not their sex alone who
suffered the vexation of being wallflowers. 'Sometimes a prince,
or two, will come to honour the Ball, and remain sitting for
over an hour without ever being led out by any lady.' In
order to remedy this, the husband of one of these ladies
'displeased at such discourtesy, will send a message to his wife
telling her to invite the prince to dance'. But here arose another difficulty. Whoever was invited to dance – whether man
or woman – was obliged, when their turn to invite someone
arrived, to repay the honour. So the wife replies that she
cannot invite so great a person as a prince, because she would
put him in the position of having to invite her back again. The
custom of returning an invitation was not used always with
discretion. Some brazen persons returned one another's invitations, not once, but again and again, so that, says Caroso,
'arising from this there are always [the same] four of five
persons dancing, with the rest watching, which is certainly
an ill thing'. Moreover, he adds, this made it appear that they
were carrying on some clandestine love affair; a suggestion
damaging to the reputation of any woman.[40]

On arriving at a ball given by a person of high rank, a lady
would first seek out her hostess. Seeing her while a little
distance off, the guest immediately made a slight curtsy,
followed by a deeper one on approaching nearer and at the

[40] *Della Nobiltà di Dame.*

same time making a pretence of kissing her hostess's hand. Should it happen that the hostess was of greatly superior rank to herself, the guest would pretend to kiss her knee. If circumstances did not permit the hostess to return these compliments, 'she must pretend to raise [her guest] by the hands' – indicated by a gesture towards her visitor. Whatever the disparity in rank, 'she who is visited', said Caroso, 'ought always to give every sort of welcome and caress to the lady who visits her'. It was therefore the place of the great lady to give the right-hand side to her guest, taking her visitor's left hand in her own right hand. It was good manners for the guest to demur a little, but not too much, on being given this honour. Della Casa said: 'They be also very tedious to men, and their conversation and manners are very troublesome, who show too base and abject a mind in their doings. And where the chiefest and highest place is apparently due unto them, they will ever creep down to the lowest. And it is a spiteful business to thrust them up; for they will straight jog back again, like a restive Jade, or a nag that startleth aside at his shadow.'[41]

When dancing, as at all times when a gentleman appeared in public, it was usual to wear both rapier and cloak. The cloak sometimes consisted of a long piece of material which could be worn in various ways. The short cape could hang evenly at the back, from the shoulders, or be worn over the left shoulder, leaving the sword arm free. In England it was the practice to lay aside the cloak and rapier when performing the more violent dances in which men used very vigorous steps. It seems that in Italy this would not have been wise for, says Caroso, if a dancer arranged his cloak carelessly, so that it enveloped his sword, he might imperil his life, through his inability to unsheathe it speedily.

Any lady who seated herself with others in a ballroom, did so knowing that if she was asked to dance, she should never refuse. 'A well-bred damsel never refuses him who does her this honour, of leading her out to dance; and if she does, she is deemed foolish, for if she does not wish to dance, she should not place herself in line with the others.'[42] If she had no intention of dancing, she made known her wish by keeping a

41 Della Casa: *Galateo*. London, 1576.
42 Thoinot Arbeau (Jean Tarbourot): *Orchésographie*. Langres, 1588.

veil, or some head-cloth, on her head. If pressed, against her wish, to dance, she should go away to an inner room, and in thus being obliged to refuse an invitation, the fault was not hers, but of whosoever made the mistake of asking her. It was not proper for any person, whoever it might be, to invite a lady to dance if she sat with a veil on her head. Should she remove it, while continuing to sit amongst those who were gathered for the purpose of dancing, she would be regarded as silly and badly behaved.

Some women, it seems, were careless in making certain that their farthingales, and garters tied round the leg above the knee, were securely fastened. Such things, says Caroso, 'with my own eyes I have seen fall and have to be picked up'.

CHAPTER IV

The Seventeenth Century

(a) DEPORTMENT AND ETIQUETTE

THE CAVALIER

At the beginning of the seventeenth century men were still wearing doublet and hose, legacies of the Middle Ages. By the reign of Charles I, the padded, stiffened doublets, starched ruffs, and close-cut hair had given way to loose-fitting doublets, falling lace collars, and flowing hair (Plates X*a*, and *c*, XV*a*). At the end of the century, the counterpart of modern dress for men had made its appearance, consisting of shirt, breeches, waistcoat, and coat.

Men's taste and habits in numerous other spheres appeared likewise to foreshadow modern life and thought, so that the seventeenth century produced works on good manners, some of which echoed familiar precepts from the earlier age, while others formulated rules of behaviour which were to be copied by succeeding generations.

Fashionable airs

Perhaps because rules of etiquette practised throughout the century attained a zenith of artificial complexity, more sophisticated persons cloaked their affectations behind an air of studied nonchalance which deceived no one. The cloak, carelessly draped as if about to slip off the shoulder would, by a sudden fall, reveal the rich lining. The fringed and embroidered cuffs of gauntlets were displayed better by being held negligently in the fingers (Plate X*c*). Men's wealth was still carried largely upon their persons.

The introduction of foreign fashions by those who returned from the Grand Tour, bringing with them 'some Outlandish habit . . . more affected than our owne', became the target for wits. The practised courtier developed fashionable mannerisms to aid his self-assurance, assisted by trifles carried on his person – pomander or scent-bottle, pieces of jewellery to finger; in the earlier years of the century, a fan; even the locks of his own hair falling round his shoulders, sometimes set in a carefully placed curl – 'a long Lock he has got, and the art to frizzle it; a Ring in a String and the tricke to handle it'.

Courtiers who behaved with such 'Apish formality' that they could not 'for a world discourse of ought without some mimick gesture', earned the censure of contemporary moralists. Amongst the advice offered in the spate of civility-books was the cultivation of an air of self-assurance when in company, an attribute inseparable from the behaviour of cultured persons at all times and in all ages. The seventeenth-century cavalier was reminded when in company, that if he should 'sit still and say nothing, he must be sure to have an assured countenance, not gnawing anything in his mouth, nor playing with his legs, toes or fingers'; moreover, that he should have 'always an ear and an eye about him', to hear what was being said and to be ready to join in the conversation if addressed.

Carriage of the body

A tutor of this period was as much concerned with the bodily carriage of his pupil as with the instruction of his mind. 'I will have a (dancing) Master to teach a Gentleman how to keep his body in a good posture when he stands, sitteth or walketh', wrote one who had been 'Tutor Abroad to several of the Nobility and Gentry'; 'how to come in or go out of a Chamber where is Company; he must be taught how to carry his head, his hands, and his toes out, all in the best way, and with the handsome presence. In a word, how to do things with a *Bonne Grace*, and in the finest and most genteel manner that a person is capable of. But both nature and art must concur to give a man a fair presence, which for certain is a great advantage. A Master teaches the steps, but the Grace, the carriage, and the free motion of the body must chiefly come from use.'[1]

Most treatises of deportment from the seventeenth to the nineteenth century stress the importance of 'turning the toes

[1] Jean Gailhard: *The Compleat Gentleman*. London, 1678.

outward', by which was meant a turning outwards of the leg from the hip. With many adults and older children (though not infants) this is a natural posture. To stand with the heels touching and the toes a little separated provides a broader base for the body, giving an easier balance, like standing to attention in military drill. What was termed a handsome 'carriage of the leg', or the turning outwards of the thigh and foot, came to be regarded as a necessity of elegant bearing, in contrast to the untutored, unpolished mode of the simple folk. Since deportment and dancing went hand in hand, this fashion of 'carrying the leg' influenced the steps then in use. The influence can be seen still in the technique of classical ballet, which uses the same principle of 'turn-out' as the basis for its movement today. To walk in a 'splay-footed' fashion, arose from forcing out the feet alone from the ankle instead of turning out the thigh. Clearly this was not the intention of such instruction and was condemned from the time of Della Casa to the nineteenth century. We have seen already that types of shoe affect walking, so that, from the time of James I of England, the introduction of heeled shoes for both men and women would have had an effect upon posture and movement.

Walking

A good deal of attention was paid to the manner of walking; how to walk well, and what actions to avoid. Familiar censorious observation from the days of his ancestors still follow the fashion-loving gallant as he strolls the streets, anxious that his appearance shall commend him in the eyes of those persons whose opinions he values. 'Take very good heed,' reiterates Cleland, the tutor, in 1607, 'unto your feet, and consider with what grace and countenance ye walk, so that ye go not softly tripping like a wanton maid, nor yet striding with great long paces. . . . Walk man-like with a grave, civil pace, as becometh one of your birth and age. Away with all affectation.' He must shun, likewise, the manner of those who find it hard to 'go forward one step without looking down to the rose upon their shoes; or lifting up their head to set out their band or setting up the brim of their hat'.[2]

2 James Cleland: *Hero-paideia*. London, 1607.

The notion persisted that even by his walk a man could reveal his inner character. Those who put on paper their disapproval of the manners of the age were often the ones who preserved in print many of the affectations and mannerisms by which a portrait of the man of fashion of their day can be created. The strong strain of Puritan thought is revealed in the biblical style affected by some of these writers, even though, like Richard Brathwaite, they might hold Royalist sentiments. 'It is strange to observe,' he wrote, 'how the very Body expresseth the secret fantasies of the mind; . . . I have seene in this one motion, the *Gate*, such especial arguments of a proud heart. . . . But especially when Youth is imployed in ushering his Mistress, hee walkes in the street as if hee were dancing a measure. Hee verily imagines the eyes of the whole Citie are fixed on him.'[3]

Walking in company

When walking out of doors, the etiquette of giving the right-hand side to the superior, or the side next to the wall, followed the custom known from Roman times. Accompanying a person of quality, in the street or elsewhere, a gentleman observed the etiquette of giving the former 'the upper hand and not to keep exactly side by side with him, but a little behind', unless he wished to speak, when 'we step forward to give our answer – *chapeau à la main*'. Persons of quality also had a duty towards their inferiors to see that they gave the latter as little trouble as possible; for example, in avoiding unnecessary crossing from one side of the street to the other, as this caused the inferior to change from side to side of his companion 'like a managed horse'.

Loud hailing of friends and acquaintances across the street, or running to have a word with them while accompanying someone of rank, was not tolerated: 'We are only to salute them at a distance, and so that the Persons of Quality may not perceive it.' Likewise, the ancient custom of solicitous inquiry of a wayfarer as to 'whence he comes or whither he is going' was now outmoded, unless the meeting happened between friends of some standing.

[3] Richard Brathwaite: *The English Gentleman and the English Gentlewoman*. 1641.

Keeping the wall

In the event of meeting a superior, the side of the street next to the wall was to be relinquished. If the relative degree of rank or quality between the approaching parties was difficult to define, the right to keep the wall could cause some heart-burning, particularly if there happened to be witnesses who might take note of the incident, and draw inferences disparaging to the one who gave way. The youthful gallant, ushering his lady through the streets, feared nothing, says Brathwaite, 'so much as some rude encounter for the Wall, and so be discredited in the sight of his Idol'. No pen-picture has been clearer than that of John Gay's *Trivia* in 1716, a poem on *The Art of Walking the Streets of London*, in which, according to Gay, he had 'several hints' from Swift.

> Let due civilities be strictly paid.
> The wall surrender to the hooded maid;
> Nor let thy sturdy elbow's hasty rage
> Jostle the feeble steps of trembling age:
> And when the porter bends beneath his load,
> And pants for breath; clear thou the crouded road.
> But, above all, the groping blind direct,
> And from the pressing throng the lame protect.
> You'll sometimes meet a fop, of nicest tread,
> Whose mantling peruke veils his empty head,
> At ev'ry step he dreads the wall to lose,
> And risques, to save a coach, his red-heel'd shoes;
> Him, like the miller, pass with caution by,
> Lest from his shoulder clouds of powder fly.
> But when the bully, with assuming pace,
> Cocks his broad hat, edg'd round with tarnish'd lace,

PLATE VII

a. Kneeling and offering the hand. (*Roman de la Rose.*)

b. A beggar, his hose 'broken' at the knees, doffs his cap. (*Roman de la Rose.*)

c. The meeting of the King of France with the Duke of Burgundy. Note the various hats, and the manner of holding the hands; the dais and Cloth of Estate; the kneel combined with the hand-clasp. (*Froissart.*)

d. How to take off the chaperon with scarf. (*Roman de la Rose.*)
(*Reproduced by courtesy of the Trustees of the British Museum.*)

a.

b.

c.

VII. Medieval hats.
The manner of wearing, and
of doffing them

d.

a.

b.

c.

d.

VIII.   Bows of the sixteenth and seventeenth centuries

Yield not the way; defie his strutting pride,
And thrust him to the muddy kennel's side;
He never turns again, nor dares oppose,
But mutters coward curses as he goes.

In the absence of a wall, French etiquette, copied to a great extent in England, laid down that the person of rank should be passed on his left-hand side 'to leave his right at liberty'. The same procedure was followed when travelling by coach – thus in France, passing coaches kept to the right-hand side of the road.

Not only in the streets or on journeys from one place to another was it imperative to remember to keep the correct position. A favourite pastime, either for the purpose of serious business or for pleasant recreation, was the leisurely stroll taken along the terrace, or in the court or long gallery of the spacious homes of the wealthy. The 'upper hand' in a room was not, as when out of doors, the right-hand side of the two persons who walked, but that side of the room where the great bed stood (see Plates XIc, XIVb). If the room did not contain a bed, the upper hand was that farthest from the door. This presented no difficulty when they turned at each end of the room, but where it was necessary to keep the superior always on the right-hand side, as in a garden, the inferior passed across behind his companion 'without affectation or trouble to him [to] recover the [left] side at every turn'.

PLATE VIII

a. Man and girl making a reverence. (Woodcut, about 1588, from Arbeau, *Orchésographie.*)

b. A man about to make a bow in the Italian style, by carrying the left leg backwards. The hat is held against the thigh – the usual method after doffing it. Late sixteenth century. (*Leon Palavicinius*).

c. A French nobleman of the seventeenth century bowing. He holds his hat against the left hip, having removed the right glove in order to kiss the right hand. Note the pantofles worn over heeled shoes. (*Jacques Callot.*)

d. Greeting a superior with a low bow, kissing the hand. Frontispiece to Jacques de Callières, *The Courtier's Calling* (*La Fortune des gens de qualité*), 1675.

G

Nor should the inferior stop to pluck fruit or pick flowers –
'he is to touch them only with his Eyes'. 'If', it is added,
'three be walking together, the place of Honour is in the
midst . . . the right hand is the second place, and the left
the lowest'.[4] To maintain this order on each turn, an unobtrusive change-over took place, which in the case of three
persons of equal rank, assumed an almost dance-like pattern;
each in turn changed his place with his companion. He who
had a story to tell was first given the centre position, so as to
be heard better.

Hats

A man's hat was as much a part of necessary attire as our
shoes are considered to be today. Hats were worn indoors as a
matter of course. They provided warmth against the draughts
found in large halls and in rooms with ill-fitting doors and
windows. 'Got a strange cold in my head by flinging off my
hat at a dinner', notes Pepys in his diary.

Apart from warmth, the hat was an important accessory
for the purpose of conveying the exact deference due to, or
received by, a man of any social standing whatsoever. Whether
the hat was to be removed or kept upon the head, and the
moment that it should be lifted off or returned to the head,
were considerations to be tactfully judged. Blunders made in
such circumstances were not to be lightly dismissed. Subtle
degrees of social distinction were bound up with the etiquette
of the hat.

In general, a man remained uncovered in the presence of
his superior until the latter requested him to put on his hat.
For the superior to omit making this request showed arrogance
and ill-breeding. On the other hand, if the social status of both
men was equal, for one to assume to himself the right to ask
the other to be covered made it appear as though he thought
himself the superior. In such a case, a mutual glance gave the
hint for both to cover simultaneously.

If one of greatly superior rank requested his companion to
be covered, showing his affability towards him, the inferior
could offer his thanks, yet remain uncovered if he felt it was

[4] Antoine de Courtin: *The Rules of Civility or Certain Ways of Deportment observed in France*. London, 1671.

his duty to do so; the exchange made, the best procedure was to ignore the whole question, for if the superior insisted, he might cause embarrassment to the other. For the inferior, in certain circumstances, to demur too much in complying with a request to be covered, showed tedious and ill-bred behaviour; in others, it was correct to wait for a second request. All these fine points of what was considered to be good breeding were understood by all, and the social gaffes in etiquette perpetuated by stage characters were easily appreciated by audiences of the day.

Social status was indicated, to a great extent, by dress. Apart from the aristocracy, men of the Church, lawyers, merchants, and so forth wore distinctive styles of dress, and those who merited some recognition of their position received due respect in the doffing of hats from passers-by.

On meeting a person of quality in the road, street, or else-where, an inferior would uncover. If the occasion demanded, he might even pause in his progress, remaining uncovered till the other was some distance off – the length of time or distance depended on circumstances. In those days is was not unusual to encounter members of the royal family when walking in London, as did Samuel Pepys and his companion one evening when crossing the park from St James's palace. Being dusk, says Pepys, they 'staid not to take notice' of the Duke of York and his retinue as they passed along Pall Mall, but merely continued their way across the park, whereupon one of the Duke's footmen ran after them 'looking just in our faces to see who we were' before turning away; making Pepys, as he says, 'fearful that I might not go far enough with my hat off'. On several occasions Pepys records his feelings where the etiquette of the hat concerned himself, especially when this entitled him to unaccustomed honour. In the presence of Lord Ashly, Chancellor of the Exchequer, he thought it 'mighty strange to find myself sit here in committee with my hat on, while Mr Sherwin stood bare as a clerk, with his hat off to his Lord Ashly and the rest'; but, he adds, 'I thank God I think myself never a whit the better man for all that'.[5]

Selden pointed out the folly of paying too much attention to such observances, saying 'Tis sometimes unreasonable to

[5] Samuel Peyps: *Diary.* 27 July 1663 and January 1665.

look after Respect and Reverence, either from a Man's own Servant, or Inferiors'.[6]

Royalty and the hat

The importance of the hat entered also into the politics of the day, and on occasions necessitated consultation regarding the correct procedure to be observed. No one, not even the king's own son, remained covered in the presence of royalty, with the exception of a visiting ambassador who, as representative of his royal master, was given this privilege when performing his ceremonial duties. Difficulties could, and did arise over the comparative status of various states, jealously cited by these representatives. The small states of Italy did not command a status of equal importance with that of France, Spain, or England; in consequence, the reception of ambassadors from the former had to be considered with tact and care.

Questions of this kind were among the duties of the Master of Ceremonies, and from the records of Sir John Finett who held this position between 1625 and 1641, we learn of the importance which was attached to such points of court etiquette. Kings Charles I, about to receive in audience the Ambassador Extraordinary from the Duke of Mantua, Pompeio Strozzi, was uncertain whether or not it would be politic to invite Strozzi to cover in his presence. Finett replied that when Strozzi had been received in Paris, the King of France (who at the time was ill) had not only called Strozzi to his bedside, but had commanded him to replace his hat and even to be seated. 'But,' replied Charles, 'I know that the King of Spain doth not allow the Duke of Mantua's ambassador to be covered in his presence.' To this Finett answered that that might be due to 'the supercilious and affected greatness of that King beyond all others', for his behaviour to others had been equally arrogant. 'Well,' said Charles, 'then I know what to do, bring him to me.' After receiving the formal compliments tendered by the ambassador, King Charles invited him to cover. On another occasion, King Charles stood bare-headed while he conversed with an ambassador, purposely keeping off his own hat

[6] E. Rhys (Ed.): John Selden: *Table Talk*. 1686. In *Table Talk from Ben Jonson to Leigh Hunt*. Everyman. London, 1934.

so that the other could not replace his, nor was it obligatory for the king to invite him to do so.[7]

The question of who was invited to be covered, and who not, inspired whispered gossip around the royal court; should the Prince (later Charles II), who normally would appear bareheaded in his father's presence, be invited to cover while dining, seeing that one below his station, the visiting ambassador, would wear his hat at dinner? When the prince returned as king to the throne of England, all who were present at a ball noted the command to cover given by his majesty to his natural son, the Duke of Monmouth, although he was partnering the queen.

Method of holding the hat

After removing the hat with the right hand, it was held 'not on the thigh as was formerly the custom' (as described in the previous age by Caroso) but 'in front of the busk of the pourpoint with the left hand in order to leave the other free'.[8] Sometimes it was placed under the left arm, but always with a negligent air; a too precise manner was now regarded as lacking gentility. The old-fashioned style of holding the hat down against the thigh can be seen in portraits of the period, but this method is neither as convenient nor as elegant with the large-brimmed beaver as it appeared with the small silk or velvet cap of the sixteenth century (Plates VIIIc and d, XIb, XIVa).

Smoking and snuff-taking

Tobacco in the form of pipe-smoking (Plate XIc), and particularly snuff, were widely used during this century (Fig. 3). The period was renowned for craftsmanship in snuff-boxes, made from costly materials. At first, snuff-takers carried with them a roll of tobacco and a grater called a 'Rap' (from the French râper, to scrape) in the belief that freshly grated snuff was essential. The rap had a small spoon at one end, and a little box at the other. Women especially favoured the use

[7] Sir John Finett: *Finetti Philoxenis. Some choice observations of——, Knight and Master of Ceremonies to the two last Kings.* London, 1656.

[8] Joan Wildeblood (Ed.): F. De Lauze: *Apologie de la Danse.* 1623. London, 1952.

FIG. 3   A cavalier taking snuff. Engraving after Jean Dieu
de Saint-Jean: *Prints of Costume*, 1686–7. (*British Museum*)

of the tiny spoon as this helped to keep the nails clean, while
the passion for snuff-taking drew forth the jibe that they
fed 'their very nostrils with a spoone'. Later, the grater and
box became separated, the former being left at home for the
use, no doubt, of servants or others who kept the snuff-boxes
regularly filled.

Snuff-taking had its own etiquette: 'We are not to take
snuff before any person of honour (who has privilege to take
it before us) unless he presents it himself; in that case it is

lawful, and though we have an aversion to it, we are bound to accept and pretend to make use of it.'[9]

Sneezing

If when taking snuff, or at any other time, an honourable person chanced to sneeze, the ancient custom of calling upon the deity and baring the head was still observed, though with a degree of restraint: 'We must not cry out "God bless you" with any considerable loudness, but pull off our hat, make our reverence and speak that benediction to ourselves.'[9]

Gloves

Gloves, or rather gauntlets, were less tight-fitting in this period. A correctly dressed gentleman always wore or carried gloves, and was careful to observe the latest etiquette. For example, the earlier fashion of removing the glove before offering a hand to a lady was now out of date. Before offering to lead a lady in a dance, or out of courtesy, the cavalier put on his glove; if invited by her, he was to do this quietly and without keeping her waiting.

Leading the lady

In ordinary circumstances, the man offered his right hand (Plate IIIc), the exception being that the woman was given the side of the street next to the wall when walking in a town. Should a third party join the couple, due attention had to be paid to their respective ranks. If it happened to be a man of higher quality, the first gentleman relinquished his position so that the newcomer (if he wished) could lead the lady; if the third party was another lady, the gentleman took the centre place leading either his first lady, or the other, depending upon which was of higher degree.

Kissing the hand

When either giving or receiving an object by hand, it was correct for both the giver and the receiver to remove the right-hand glove, and to kiss, or perform the gesture of kissing, the hand (Plate VIIIc and d).

[9] Courtin: *The Rules of Civility*. London, 1671.

THE CAVALIER'S LADY

The impression gained from contemporary sources suggests that the fashionable Elizabethan woman often resembled a wooden image in appearance and deportment. Her clothes disguised her natural, feminine shape; she wore artificial hair, dyed or bleached to an unnatural shade; her face was painted to the extent that it seemed that she dared hardly smile; she had to be reminded that she should not sit still like an image.

With the wider introduction of French fashions on the accession of Charles I, women's dress presented a greater simplicity and elegance (Plate Xb), and this was matched by a desire to acquire in her bearing an appearance of greater ease, and at least a seeming naturalness. The erect attitude of the body was assisted still by the firmly corseted bodice, but as this was now partly concealed by the skirt of the gown which was worn over the bodice, the impression made on the beholder is one of less rigidity. Softly billowing skirts took the place of the cage-like farthingales, moving gently with the gracious rustle of silk or satin. For the first time in women's fashions in Europe, the full sleeves, finishing just below the elbow, revealed a portion of the arm. The low-cut bodice gave freedom of movement to head and neck, neither of which were encumbered any longer with large head-dresses, veils or high ruffs. The deep collar favoured by some, particularly the Puritans, and the hooded cape worn by all when out of doors, were garments both practical and easy to wear. Heeled shoes, in style similar to those worn by men, were to remain for many decades, as did the patten and pantofle.

Good manners and deportment were still regarded as the most necessary accomplishments for women. It was considered unsuitable for them to strive after intellectual pursuits. Learning was confined to those arts which would embellish their persons, or aid their proficiency in running their home establishments. Even those who, later in the century, put in a plea for better education for women, were forced to submit to the conventions of the day that 'Women ought to be brought up to a comely and decent carriage, to their Needle, to Neatness, to understand all those things that do particularly belong to their sex'; but, continued the writer 'meerely to teach Gentle-

women to Frisk and Dance, to paint their Faces, to curl their
Hair, to put on a Whisk, or wear gay Clothes, is not truly to
adorn . . . their Bodies'.[10]

Attempts to present women on a more elevated plane
dwelt more on their outward charms than their mental ability,
as in a work dated 1677. This agrees that women cannot com-
pare with men in 'External Advantage, as Sciences and
Authority', nevertheless they 'have this Advantage: that the
Eloquence of Action is in them much more lively than in
Men . . . and their Air is noble and great, their Port free and
Majestic, their Carriage decent, their Gestures natural, their
Style engaging, their Words easie, and their Voice sweet and
melting.'[11]

Despite this praise, women, as well as men, had their severe
critics. 'For your Carriage, it should neither be too precise,
nor too loose', writes Brathwaite, who advised women to endeavour to make 'their smile pleasing, mixt with bashfulness;
their pace graceful, without too much activeness; their whole
posture delightful with a seemly carelessness'. During the
seventeenth century, affectation of behaviour attracted the
attention of many who described the manners of their fellow
men – and women. Scorn was poured upon those women whose
assumed affectation made them 'set their looke, gait, and
whatsoever else . . . so punctually as if they had entered a
solemn Contract with eye, face, hand, foot and all'. The lady
who found herself at court was assailed on all sides by the artificial extravaganzas of the courtly modes of her associates,
where one gallant would make a set speech to her glove and
another would create a great occasion out of holding her muff
or her fan while she pinned on her mask. She was reminded
that the ephemeral popularity of the court was like glass –
'bright but brittle' – where courtiers were compared to
counters, worth so much one day, and cast aside the next.

John Evelyn, writing in sorrow of the death of his daughter
Mary in 1685, describes a cultured and charming girl of those
days as one who possessed grace and ability in the arts of pleas-

[10] B. Makin: *An Essay to Revive the Ancient Education of Gentlewomen
in Religion, Manners, Arts and Tongues.* London, 1673.
[11] *The Woman as Good as the Man, or the Equality of Both Sexes.*
Trans. from the French of F. Poulain de La Barre, by A.L., 1677.

ing the eye and the ear. Her outward graces had been a great
pride to Evelyn: 'The justness of her stature, person, comeli-
ness of countenance, gracefulness of motion, unaffected, though
more than ordinary beautiful. . . .' She sang well and played the
harpsichord equally well, and when she sang 'it was as charming to the eyes as to the ear', having learned from the two well-
known teachers, Signors Pietro and Bartholomeo.[12]

It was not then thought appropriate for a girl of good
family to act or dance before anyone except intimate friends
or relations, but her 'talent of rehearsing any comical part or
poem . . . was more pleasing than heard on the theatre'. Her
dancing master was the well-known Monsieur Isaac who had
taught at the English court in the early eighteenth century. In
an age when every man and woman learned to dance as a
matter of education, Evelyn was confident Isaac agreed that
Mary 'danced with the greatest grace'. Although this talent in
dancing might not have been much displayed, the effect upon
her deportment showed in 'the gracefulness of her carriage,
which was with an air of sprightly modesty not easily to be
described. Nothing affected, but natural and easy as well in her
deportment as in her discourse.'

Poise

A treatise of dance and deportment of the early seventeenth
century emphasizes that if the head is well placed, the poise of
the body will be correct. In the case of women this was regarded as especially important, for, it was said, 'the face of
the Lady is the first object which draws the eyes of the beholders'. The dancing master, therefore, was advised to pay
attention to the proper bearing of her head.[13]

Walking

It was the duty of the dancing master to teach his pupils
the correct manner of walking. With the master holding her
hands, the lady was to be taught to 'put her feet close to one
another, the toes outward . . . sedately and in a straight line'.

A visit to the market was an important event, and here a
lady or gentlewoman of good birth was accompanied, if not by

[12] Evelyn: *Diary*. Everyman, 1930. Vol. II. pp. 217–18.
[13] Wildeblood (Ed.): De Lauze: *Apologie de la Danse*. 1623.

FIG. 4   Lady wearing a mask. Her gown is tucked up and she carries a muff. Hollar: *Ornatus Muliebris Anglicanus, or These Severall Habits of Englishwomen from the Nobility to the Country Woman as they are in these times.* London, 1640. (*British Museum*)

her own family, at least by her usher and perhaps a maid and a page; a small, sedate group appearing like a tiny, secluded island, as they moved with restrained deportment through the hurly-burly of surrounding stalls, live farmyard produce, vegetables, and hardware of all kinds, amid the noise and arguments of hard bargaining (Plate IIIc).

Walking out of doors, the outer gown was often tucked up to keep it clear of the ground (Fig. 4). Ladies' gowns no longer bore the long trains that were in vogue during the previous centuries, except on state or court occasions. Unless the gown

FIG. 5   A lady's smaller train carried by a page. Engraving
after Jean Dieu de Saint-Jean: *Prints of Costume*, 1686–7.
(*British Museum*)

was tucked up, the smaller trains now worn required carrying
when out of doors. As in medieval times, etiquette decreed that
a lady should not have her train carried in the presence of
another of higher condition. The tucked-up gown was a necessary custom in foul weather, with ill-paved streets, but to
appear thus was in some circumstances regarded as impolite,
and even immodest.

Leading by the hand
    The polite manner of conducting a lady was for the man to
offer her his hand (Plate IIIc); this could be regarded as an

honour shown to the woman, or, if her rank was above his, as an honour given to the man. 'Thence to my house,' wrote Samuel Pepys, 'where I took great pride to lead [Lady Carteret] through the Court by the hand, she being very fine, and her page carrying up her train'[14] (Fig. 5). According to Pepys, young Mr Carteret, in manners of etiquette of this nature, was 'the most awkward man I ever met with in my life'. Pepys attempted to improve the young man's manners, spending 'an hour or two' in the gallery. 'Here I taught him what to do: to take the lady always by the hand to lead her', besides paying her the customary verbal compliments used by all in this period. However, Mr Carteret was not a good pupil, for when the whole family returned from church by coach, he had not 'the confidence to take his lady once by the hand, coming or going, which I told him of'.[15]

Masks

Ladies who did not care to be recognized in the street or any public place, covered their faces with a mask (Figs. 4 and 6). It was uncivil to keep on the mask if they were saluted by someone they met in the street, unless the exchange of salutations was performed some distance apart. In the presence of royalty, whether at a distance or near by, it would have been very remiss to keep on the mask. The theatre was one of the places where women of good family often wished to remain disguised. 'To the Royal Theatre,' said Pepys. 'Here I saw my Lord Falconbridge and his lady, my Lady Mary Cromwell . . . when the house began to fill, she put on her vizard, and so kept it on all the play; which of late is become a great fashion among the ladies, which hides their whole face.'[16]

(b) SALUTATIONS

The Bow

The transition of the bow from the medieval to the modern can be seen during the seventeenth century. Until almost the end of the century men continued to bend both knees while

14 Pepys: *Diary*. 30 June 1662.
15 ibid., 15 and 16 July 1665.
16 ibid., 12 June 1663.

making their bows, but this bending of the knees had become subsidiary to the bowing of the body.

> Observe in Curtesie to take
> a rule of decent kinde,
> Bend not thy body too far foorth,
> nor backe thy leg behind.[17]

We see here the bow in the old-fashioned style, where the leg was carried backwards (but not too far), and the body could be inclined forward (but not too much).

During the sixteenth century, 'yealding, bending, and bowing' the body when making a reverence became the style for men of fashion. Gallants who returned from the Grand Tour, having 'travell'd to make legs, and seen the cringe of several courts and courtiers', were mocked by their conservative contemporaries.

We have seen how the figure of speech, 'to bow and scrape', arose from the backward scraping of the foot described by Caroso. Towards the end of the sixteenth century another figure of speech makes its appearance in the literature of the day – to 'make a leg'. In *All's Well That Ends Well* (1595), Clown speaks of making a 'leg', and here the expression is used in its contemporary sense, but as put in the mouth of King Richard III – 'You make a leg, and Bolingbroke says ay', it is an example of how playwrights as well as actors used the manners of their own time, irrespective of period. It is clear from contemporary illustrations and from literary sources, that, in making bows, the old style of half-kneel was not immediately replaced by the new style 'making of legs'. As in all changes of fashion, both methods would have prevailed until by degrees the older style was superseded.

The main difference between Caroso's bow and that shown by De Lauze, was that the leg was now moved forward, thereby producing the effect known as 'making a leg', whereas formerly the leg had been carried backwards. This deliberate placing forward of the leg, on commencing the bow, carries with it a certain self-consciousness so typical of the studied behaviour of this period, an attitude absent from the simple medieval

---

[17] *The Boke of Demeanor* by Richard Weste. 1619. In *Early English Meals and Manners*. E.E.T.S. London, 1868.

reverence. 'Former times were not so jaded as to fashions,' cried Richard Brathwaite in 1630, '. . . legges were held for useful supporters, but no Complemental postures.'

The fashionable world now turned their eyes to the French court to seek guidance on social etiquette. The extreme forward inclination of the body used in the new bow appears to have been associated with French manners: 'Remember kissing of your hand and answering with the French time, and flexure of your body.'[18] There is also the courtier who 'salutes a friend as if he had a stitch'[19] (Plate VIII*d*).

Previous to the seventeenth century, authors of instructional books on manners found it sufficient to devote to the reverence a single description, making it understood that the depth of the movement could be profound or not, according to circumstances. When performed to royalty the reverence would be deeper than that used in normal contacts. From the seventeenth century, however, subtle distinctions of time, place, and the quality of the persons present, created the need for more specific instruction.

The slighter bow, used informally when meeting or passing by can be defined as little more than a pause in walking (Appendix I*c*(i)), whereas when saluting persons of 'quality', the full inclination of the body forward, together with the kissing of the right hand, changed the action into one of deep respect (Appendix I*c*(ii)). (Plate VIII*d*).

This flowing bow was as much an expression of the age as were the softly-falling lace collars, curling feathers, and hanging ribbons with which the cavaliers loved to deck themselves. The sweeping arm, the curving back, these matched the current phrase then used in salutation – 'Your humble servant' – said to have been introduced in imitation of French manners then in vogue.

The Rules of Civility, a well-known treatise of contemporary manners, was translated into English in 1671 from the French of Antoine de Courtin. On the important matter of making bows, the spirited advice offered by de Courtin becomes a clearer picture when combined with the technical description given by De Lauze: 'If we be to salute any person arrived

---

18 Ben Jonson: *The Devil is an Ass*. Act III. i.
19 idem. *Cynthia's Revels*. Act III. ii.

lately out of the Country, it must be done with a humble in-
flexion of our bodies, taking off our Glove, and putting our
hand down to the ground. But above all, we are not to do it
precipitously, nor with over much pains, neither throwing ourselves hastily upon our Nose, nor rising up again too suddenly,
but gently and by degrees; lest the person saluted, bowing at
the same time to you, might have his teeth beaten out by the
throwing up [of] your head.'[20] In 1685 an augmented version
of de Courtin's book repeats the same advice, and as late as
1719 the Scotsman, Adam Petrie, adds that it should be the
back of the hand which is lowered towards the ground.

The Curtsy

For the first time, the reverence of the man was distinct from
that of the woman; the bow consisted in bowing the body, the
curtsy in bending the knees.

The curtsy was also made in two different ways; the one
used for a passing salutation, and the other for the salutation
made on entering or leaving a room, for greeting persons of
quality and when beginning or finishing a dance (Appendix
I(c) iii and iv).

Practice makes perfect, and familiarity gives assurance, for
only thus could these stately ladies, balanced on their toes in
the manner of a gymnast in a 'knee-bend', perform deep curtsies
with due elegance. With the body held erect and very slightly
inclined forward, the lady gently and steadily bent her knees
outwards, lifting the heels off the ground only if the curtsy
was required to be made low; the arms were held easily at

[20] Courtin, op. cit.

PLATE IX

a. and b. Commencing and finishing the bow. (L. P. Boitard.)

c. The forward bow made in presenting a book. In this instance
the hat is kept under the left arm. (L. P. Boitard.)

d. The bow sideways, with the corresponding curtsy. (G. van der
Gucht).

e. The curtsy with the feet in the First Position. Note the position
of the hands and fan. Note also (and in d) the erect posture of the
body. (L. P. Boitard.) (Reproduced by courtesy of the Trustees of
the British Museum.)

b.   c.

d.   e.

IX.   The eighteenth-century bow and curtsy

a.

b.

c.

d.

e.

f.

X. Elegance in standing

each side. The eyes, which should look at the company or person, at the moment when the curtsy was first 'directed' were lowered (but not the head) on the knee-bend, and raised again as the body regained the upright position. It must be remembered that while greetings, adieus, and conversation, were punctuated by bows or curtsies, these reverences were not made low to the ground, for this would create tedious and even ridiculous interruptions. Therefore, in general, a suffic-iently deep curtsy could be made while keeping both heels on the ground, particularly with the higher heels then in fashion.

Kissing the hand

This fashion remained throughout the Restoration period, both as an accompaniment to a bow and as a gesture of courtesy when handing, or receiving, any object to or from a person of quality: 'You must always pull off your Glove, and kiss your hand when you take from or present anything to, a person of Quality, or when you return anything to them.' But the person of quality was not to be kept waiting, so that the correct procedure was to hand the object first and after-wards 'not to forget to kiss your hand'.[21]

[21] ibid.

PLATE X

a. James, 1st Duke of Hamilton. *Daniel Mytens. (Reproduced by permission of The Duke of Hamilton.)*

b. Lady Penelope Wriothesley. A posture seen often in portraits of the seventeenth century. *Van Dyck. (Reproduced by permission of The Earl of Spencer, from the collection at Althorp.)*

c. Lords John and Bernard Stuart. Note the carelessly draped cloaks and the gloves. Also (as in *a*), the pantofles, the falling lace at the neck and edging the boot-hose, and the natural, flowing hair. *Van Dyck. (Reproduced by permission of The Earl Mountbatten of Burma.)*

d. 'To stand genteel'. *L. P. Boitard,* eighteenth century. *(Reproduced by courtesy of the British Museum.)*

e. The lady's posture when walking or standing. *L. P. Boitard. (Reproduced by courtesy of the British Museum.)*

f. An example of the correct posture for a young lady of the nineteenth century, except for the feet which are shown too much turned outwards. *The Young Lady's Book, 1829.*

H

The Embrace

Towards the close of the seventeenth century the embrace
as a custom of salutation began to go out of fashion in England.
But as is usually the case, the country squire and his lady
were slower to change their ways than were the fashionable
town gallants. 'You think you're in the country, where great
lubberly brothers slabber and kiss one another when they
meet,' says Witwoud to Sir Wilful in William Congreve's *The
Way of the World*. ''Tis not the fashion here; 'tis not indeed
dear brother.'[22] In the same scene, the stage direction to Sir
Wilful, 'salutes [Mrs] Marwood', is accompanied by this question, 'No offence, I hope'. To which she replies, 'No, sure, Sir'.
Her reaction reveals that not only between men but also
between the sexes this fashion of salutation was becoming
outmoded.

But there is plenty of evidence that it was not the French
alone who had retained this ancient custom in the early years
of the century. In 1623 Sir John Finett was commissioned to
carry important news to Prince Charles, then in Spain. Having
arrived at the coast and ridden on horseback throughout the
night with his companion, he delivered his message to the con-
tentment, he says, of the Duke of Buckingham who, to express
his thanks, kissed Finett, presenting him with a diamond ring
which he drew from his own finger 'of above an hundred
pounds in valew'.

For remaining at his post in London during the terrible re-
currence of the plague in the summer and autumn of 1665
when the court and all else who could do so had fled from the
city, Sir John Evelyn recalls the gratitude expressed to himself
by both the King and the Duke of Albemarle; the former by
giving 'in a most gracious manner' his hand to Evelyn to kiss,
and the duke who 'came towards me, and embraced me with
much kindness, telling me if he had thought my danger would
have been so great he would not have suffered his Majesty to
employ me in that station.'[23]

That other famous diarist, Samuel Pepys, records a similar

[22] William Congreve: *The Way of the World*. Act III. xv, in *Restoration Plays*. Everyman, Dent. London, 1932.
[23] Evelyn: *Diary*. Vol. II. p. 2.

FIG. 6   A lady out walking, wearing a cape, hood, muff
and mask. Hollar: *Ornatus, Muliebris Anglicanus, or The
Severall Habits of Englishwomen from the Nobility to the
Country Woman as they are in these times*. London, 1640.
(*British Museum*)

honour paid to his cousin, Admiral Sir Edward Montague, later
Earl Sandwich, by King Charles who, on his journey to
London in 1660 'did with a great deal of affection kiss my Lord
[Montagu] upon his first meeting'. Pepys's friend, Sir George
Carteret, treasurer of the Navy from 1661–7, with his wife,
Lady Carteret, bade Pepys a friendly family farewell. Sir
George, says Pepys in 1665, 'kissed me himself heartily; and
my Lady several times, with great kindness, and then the young
ladies, and so, with much joy, bade "God be with you" '.[24]

[24] Pepys: *Diary*. August 1665.

After making a deep bow, and kissing his own hand to a lady, the gentleman then kissed the lady, but this was only if she made the first advance. When out walking the lady wore a cape and hood and, if she was a lady of quality who thus offered her cheek, the man was 'only to pretend to salute her by putting [his] head to her Hoods' (Fig. 6). In France it was the practice to 'salute Ladies on the Cheek'. In Britain and Ireland they saluted them on the lips − 'but Ladies gave their Inferiors their Cheek only'.

If there happened to be other ladies in attendance on the lady of quality they were not to be saluted until they were no longer in the presence of their superiors, 'and then you may salute them, with an Apology', for previously being obliged to ignore them.[25]

Foreign visitors to England in earlier periods had commented on the prevalence of the custom of kissing. So general was the practice, that when Charles II travelled towards London to retake the throne,'the country gentlewomen' says Pepys, did hold up their heads to be kissed by the King, not taking his hand to kiss, as they should do'. Pepys, himself, promised his wife he would refrain from kissing the ladies 'after the first' − the kiss of salutation. 'It is undecent to kiss Ladies but in Civility,' wrote Petrie nearly fifty years later, although Pepys's merry ways were not so uncommon in Stuart England.

'It has, for a length of time, been customary to salute the ladies upon a first introduction to them'; declared *The New Chesterfield* in 1830, 'but these liberties having occasioned, at times, a great deal of unhappiness, the custom is dropped in polite companies, and a well-bred man now never attempts it. He introduces himself only with a distant bow.'[26]

(c) HOSTS AND GUESTS

Festivities, public and private, continued to occupy a great part of the lives of men and women who moved in and around court circles. Balls, private dancing parties, masques presented at court and by wealthy landowners, plays, and various games

[25] Adam Petrie: *Rules of Good Deportment, or of Good Breeding*. Edinburgh, 1719.
[26] Earl of Car: *The New Chesterfield*. London, 1830.

of skill or chance were among these amusements. In addition, the practice of paying courtesy visits increased gradually in social importance. 'As to the visits which we are to make, if we would follow the Example of some People, who make them the whole business of their lives, we have nothing to do but go from one House to another.'[27] This particular form of social duty must have weighed heavily upon those who found such tedious punctilios hard to endure.

The courtesy visit, however, was an established social institution, and no man of good breeding would omit this duty, if only to comply with common etiquette. Where it was prompted by genuine friendship, time would pass pleasantly enough, but where expediency was the compelling motive there was need to resort to niceties of polite conduct. 'For example, a great person is to be visited often, and his health to be inquired after, if for no other end but to preserve ourselves in his favour. And every time he has an eminent occasion of joy or of sadness, we are to congratulate, or condole.'[27] Examples of set speeches to assist those unpractised in this form of flattery were printed in *The Academy of Complements*, which appeared in numerous editions from 1640 into the eighteenth century.

Advice on how to behave on these occasions form a substantial portion of the books of civility of this period. Obligations of this nature at times fell to the lot of those who were unversed in the correct manner of entering or leaving a room, of where and how to sit, and what subjects of conversation were considered most suitable.

Preparation for the visit

When visiting ladies or persons of quality, the first thing to be considered was how to arrive with one's clothes and person in a presentable and clean condition. Nothing would be worse than to enter with boots covered with the filth and mire of the roads or streets, and clothes muddied from the splashing of carriages and of animals' hooves. To be obliged, in such a state, to walk upon rich carpets and to sit upon velvet chairs, would be distressing both to visitor and host. To change

[27] Antoine de Courtin: *The Rules of Civility*.

one's boots on arrival at the door was regarded as little better than to enter covered in dirt, as this gave the impression that the visitor was too poor to provide himself with a suitable form of conveyance.

Amongst the French nobility of this age, it was almost a vice to be poor, or at least to reveal one's poverty to the world. But a gentleman would not be thought sufficiently agreeable to be received into polite society by merely providing himself with a carriage, horse, or sedan-chair. Though to our modern notions the standards of seventeenth-century cleanliness were low, there were limits to personal negligence. It is, in fact, unnecessary to depend upon baths to be clean. It depends upon the amount of washing done, and here opinions have varied – and still vary – on what is necessary. Polite society in the seventeenth century considered an occasional visit to the baths to wash the whole body was absolutely necessary. Daily ablutions appear to have been restricted to the hands, while the face was washed 'almost as often'. A gentleman would keep a *valet-de-chambre*, also a barber to shave him, though the current fashion for wearing beards minimized the latter's work. The head was washed from time to time, or at least cleaned with some good powder. The duties of servants included the cleaning of house, furniture, and clothes.

Correct etiquette

A man of good breeding would know that 'Civility is a Science', which taught men 'to dispose [their] words and actions in their proper and just places'. This depended upon four things: 'Our own age. The quality of the person with whom we converse. The time, and the place of our Conversation.' Having thus prepared himself, it remained only for the gentleman to consider the circumstances of his visit. Ambassadors, and persons who were occupied in private or public business, were not expected to receive visitors during the morning; nor were those who had been recently bereaved; nor those who were ill – unless they could 'sit up in their beds and put on their upper garments', it being the custom to lie naked in bed. There were, to be sure, some persons – described in their day as 'Nice, Affected Beaux' – who preferred to receive their visitors while they lay in bed; reserving the hours between ten and twelve in the morning for this purpose, where they would be found reclining 'most magnificently, with a long Perriwig neatly laid over the Sheets, extravagantly powdered, and exactly curled'. Nor was it polite to call upon women in the morning. The good housewife would have much to employ her during these hours, while the idle society lady would prefer to recoup some of the lost hours of sleep.

Entering the room

Should the gentleman arrive at the door leading to the inner chamber of some prince or great noble, there being no one present to announce him, he must remember on no account to knock more than once – in some circumstances it was uncivil to knock at all. For instance, it was accounted 'no less that brutish' to knock at the door leading to the chief bed-chamber – 'the way is to scratch only with the nails'. Having made known his presence, the usher of the chamber would appear to inquire the visitor's name. It was correct to give only the surname, without any prefix, as 'Lord', or 'Mr'. On being admitted, he was to enter 'softly and soberly, with a profound reverence and inclination of the body'.

Reception room

The room in which guests were received was prepared in advance and arranged according to circumstance. Should the guest be one of quality, the *portière*, or hanging which covered the door on the outside, was let down. For a public audience this hanging was raised, unless the company included someone of high rank, in which case it would be lowered. Reception rooms for entertaining guests were entered by double doors, which on occasions of some importance were opened fully. A host would be accused of showing superiority if only one half was opened, unless, of course, his visitor, or visitors, were of much inferior rank. The seats in the room were set in readiness for the guests. Chairs with arms were reserved for the more honourable guests; others sat upon chairs with backs only, unless they felt it incumbent to sit upon a stool. The chair for the chief guest was placed so that it faced the entrance door, with a view of the whole room. The host's seat was set facing this, with his back to the door. Should there be several visitors who merited equal honour, their chairs were arranged one beside the other, along the wall which faced the door. If only two were present, the chairs were placed to face one another, with the entrance door to one side – 'and that on the right-hand of the door is the better place'.

Demeanour of the Visitor

It was polite to enter the room with gloves on, unless the bow of greeting entailed kissing the visitor's hand, when the right-hand glove was pulled off. This could be replaced after the visitor was seated. He did not replace his hat, unless pressed to do so by his host. At all times he was to appear at ease with a 'seeming negligence', so long as this appeared natural. Only those who were ill at ease fidgeted with their hat, gloves, neck bands, or crossed and uncrossed their legs, but 'affected negligence is worst of all'.

Spitting

In the earlier years of the century to spit upon the floor was permissible, but as richer furnishings and carpets replaced rush-strewn floors, the polite world was taught that people should 'forbear hawking or spitting as much as you can'. If unable to restrain themselves, and particularly if they 'Observe [the room] neat and kept cleanly,' they should then turn back to the company, 'and rather spit in your Handkerchief than [in] the Room.' 'To bed this night,' writes Pepys, 'having first put up a spitting sheet, which I find very convenient.' So little were people concerned with such behaviour that Pepys, being placed rather far back in a dark place at the theatre, made no objection because 'a lady spit backwards upon me by mistake, not seeing me; but after seeing her to be a very pretty lady, I was not troubled at it at all'.[28]

The Visitor departs

It was always the place of the visitor to make a move to depart, and to judge the right moment to rise. This would depend on whether or not his presence appeared welcome enough to prolong his stay. To depart abruptly in the middle of

[28] Pepys: *Diary.* 28 January 1661.

a discussion in which the company was partaking would be boorish. If his host insisted on accompanying his guest out of the room, it would be uncivil to make too great a show of wishing to decline the honour. It should be accepted with due humility and thanks. If the host wished to go as far as his own gate, and if he then could not be persuaded to return to his house, it would be impolite for the guest to enter his coach or sedan-chair in his host's presence. In this case, the visitor was forced to set off walking, commanding his coach or chair to follow, until out of sight of his noble host.

The Host's obligations

The host's duties are always more onerous than those of the visitor. Having assured himself that all was in readiness for the guest's reception, consideration of the distance he should go to meet his visitor was a delicate one. With those whose known rank made the decision easy, it was but his duty to observe the rules of precedence. With strangers from abroad whose rank was difficult to compare with the English aristocracy, it was wise to overdo the civility. One eminent person, being uncertain of the correct procedure towards a prospective guest, hit upon the convenient notion of feigning illness, thus being able to receive his guest in bed. Governors of provinces were obliged at times to travel round the country on their judicial duties. Should their route pass by the estate of someone of rank or wealth, the owner of the estate might dispatch some of his gentlemen to intercept the traveller, in order to invite him to stay a night or two, and this might mean going some nine or ten miles. If he wished to show the visitor greater honour, the host himself might accompany his gentlemen. He would not wish, however, to embarrass his guest by making too great a show of civility, so could explain his journey as being made 'under pretence of taking the air'. If the host remained at home, he might send a few more attendants to greet the company or traveller, as they drew nearer, until, when close to the house, he would set out to welcome the visitor himself. In any case, it was deemed polite for the host to dress himself as though he had intended to travel. On sighting his visitor, etiquette ruled that he should 'hasten his pace, as if he would have gone further to receive him'.

When greeting his superior, the host placed himself, as a rule, at the bottom of the stairs leading to the private chamber on the first floor. The gentlemen attendants would have been sent to the gate to give the first welcome. An equal was received at the top of the stairs, the gentlemen having met him at the bottom. The reception of persons of inferior rank depended upon their own quality, it being correct to use more rather than less courtesy toward them. The distance from the main reception chamber indicated the respect awarded them, the farther away from the chamber, the greater the respect. This was regulated according to custom, for example, as far as two or three rooms distant from the reception chamber, or in the ante-chamber, or as close as the door of the chamber itself, or the greeting might be made in the middle of the chamber.

More than one guest

If the host was occupied with one visitor, a person of inferior rank would be conducted to another room where the gentlemen ushers entertained him as he waited. If his rank was much inferior, he would be shown to an ante-chamber where a number of people assembled on such occasions. On the other hand, a person of some eminence, or of equal quality, who arrived while his host was entertaining others, would not be kept waiting. With an apology to his former guests, with whom he left one or two of his gentlemen ushers, the host went to greet the newcomer. Directly a visitor rose to depart, the host, in making a scrape or noise with his foot or chair, drew the attention of an attendant, who thereupon lifted up the door-hangings and opened the doors. If the guest merited special attention, the host went ahead to do these courtesies himself. 'If he be gouty or lame, 'tis but civil to present him with your hand.'

Lighting the way

Normally these social calls were made during daylight, but should it become dark before the visit ended, the head officer of the chamber gave orders for a torch of white wax to be taken to the footmen's office; also two white candles for each room, with possibly more in the room where the guests were being entertained. In the ante-chamber two or three were placed ready so that they could be lighted and carried by the gentlemen ushers when the guests left. In performing this service these gentlemen took care that they did not turn their backs directly upon the honoured guest. At the door of the great hall, footmen or pages were ready to carry torches to light the visitor and his attendants as far as his carriage, or through the grounds of the house. Protocol regulated the numbers or torches to be used – four if the visitor was of equal rank with his host, six for one of superior rank.

Ladies

As for ladies, who observed the same punctilios as did the men, there was the additional ceremony concerning masks, hoods, and trains of the gown. Before entering a room in which her hostess was ready to greet her, it would have been a great discourtesy to forget to remove the mask from her face, or to omit to let down the skirts of her outer robes, normally looped up away from the dirt of the streets. If she did not wish to take off her cape and hood, she was obliged at least to push back the hood from off her head.

CHAPTER V

The Eighteenth Century

(a) DEPORTMENT AND ETIQUETTE

THE GENTLEMAN

By the end of the seventeenth century the long transition from fashions and modes of life largely modelled on medieval thinking was over. Eighteenth-century ways began already to suggest the pattern of the world we know, at least in big cities such as London and Bath, where the world of fashion was concentrated.

Country gentle-folk, living their quiet yet hospitable lives, were slower to follow the new ways in manners, dress and daily habits. Looking upon these 'People of Mode in the Country', *The Spectator* found 'in them the Manners of the last Age'. The older generation, brought up to observe a tyrannically formal etiquette, were puzzled by the younger members of society who could no longer tolerate such stiff and precise behaviour.

Whereas, originally, the growth of good manners had arisen from the desire to mingle amicably with one's fellow men, the seeming difficulty mankind experiences in avoiding exaggeration and extremes led to an absurd excess of 'civilities'. Throughout the previous era these had become so burdensome that in desperation 'the Modish World', said *The Spectator*, had 'thrown most of them aside'. 'At present . . . an unconstrained Carriage, and a certain Openness of Behaviour are the height of Good Breeding. The Fashionable World is grown free and easie; our Manners sit more loose upon us. Nothing is so modish as an agreeable Negligence. . . . Good Breeding shows itself most where . . . it appears the least.'

A man who was unaccustomed to the fashionable society

of the town, it was said, could be recognized by 'his Excess of Good Breeding' – by his strict attention to the punctilios of etiquette with a too rigid and formal observance of cere-mony. 'A Polite Country Squire shall make you as many Bows in half an hour as would serve a Courtier for a Week.'[1] A most tiresome nuisance, seeing that every bow thus made had to be acknowledged with another by the recipient.

Lord Chesterfield, with great good sense, reminds his son that 'good breeding, you know, does not consist in low bows and formal ceremony'. His perpetual anxiety over his son's outward appearance and behaviour arose from his realization of their importance in the profesion for which the boy was being prepared; but anxiety was emphasized the more by the youth's natural *gaucherie*. Chesterfield wished the boy to acquire 'an easy, civil and respectful behaviour', which, he said, consisted of 'a thousand nameless little things, which nobody can describe, but which everybody feels'.[2]

Nevertheless, the new ease of behaviour lately found amongst the *avant-garde* of smart society, was easy only in comparison with the stiffness of the older generation. The numberless hints on behaviour were repeated *ad infinitum* in all authoritative works on the subject, with little variation, throughout the eighteenth century. In general, what they aimed at can be summed up as bodily discipline; thus we re-turn to the theme of medieval times. Bodily discipline concerns the whole person – the control of the features, the manner of speaking, laughing, and so forth. Those who have been reared in an atmosphere of mental and physical discipline – not necessarily of elevated birth – will reflect this in their features and actions. Whether or not this happens to be favoured by the fashion of the period is immaterial; it is the result of training which is neither unnatural nor harmful when absorbed in childhood. In the eighteenth century it would not have occurred to the younger, fashionable set to deprive their sons, much less their daughters, of the careful tuition in deportment which was left mainly to the visiting dancing master. Boys and girls were spoken of as young gentlemen and ladies.

---

[1] *The Spectator*: No. 119 (Addison) 17 July 1711. Vol. II.
[2] Earl of Chesterfield: *Letters to his Son and Others*. Everyman. London, 1938.

Accordingly their behaviour was moulded upon that of their elders, as were their clothes. Childish romping was soon laid aside and replaced by a gravity that was considered neither unnatural nor unbecoming in those of tender years. The notion that grown-ups should be expected to tolerate or condone interruptions and other nuisances committed by children, was wholly unacceptable to the normal well-disciplined family. Children could indulge their playful fancies among themselves but in the presence of their parents and elders it was expected that they should observe strict rules of decorum.

The deportment of a dancing master was regarded with certain amusement by the ordinary man, who had no wish to emulate so exact a bearing. At the same time, many valuable works on the subject of dancing and deportment owe their inception to these masters of the art of movement, for the un-professional writer on this, or any other subject, cannot hope to achieve the same command of detail. The manner of standing, walking, removing or replacing the hat, and so on, was not left to individual caprice; the right method was recorded by these masters for the benefit of their pupils – and now, for us.

Young Philip Stanhope, to whom Chesterfield's fatherly advice was directed, began his dancing lessons at the age of thirteen. 'Dancing is in itself a very trifling, silly thing,' said Chesterfield, 'but it is one of those established follies to which people of sense are sometimes obliged to conform.' Moreover, its practice would assist the lad in learning how to put on his hat in the proper manner. Three years later, the dancing lessons were still taking place, and Lord Chesterfield remarks that he will 'say nothing with regard to your bodily carriage and address, but leave them to the care of your dancing master'.

At this time much was written concerning the ill effects of restrictive clothing upon posture; for example, the tight corsets favoured by women's fashions, and the negligence of parents, tutors, and nurses towards children during childhood. John Weaver, a dancing master of repute, condemned swaddling-clothes for infants. Although this custom had been in use from biblical times, the ailments induced, said Weaver, 'often occasion not only Deformity, but even Death itself; and these proceed from the manner of Swathing our Infants'. Unless done with the greatest care, swaddling caused pressure on the ribs and chest, which affected the natural action of the lungs; also, with careless nurses, deformity of the legs and feet.[3] (Plate XIV*a*, and Fig. 7.)

FIG. 7 A mother shows a swaddled infant to its father. Seventeenth century. *Abraham de Bosse*. (*British Museum*)

Poise

Dancing masters of the eighteenth century followed the precept suggested by De Lauze in 1623, that the first rule of importance in acquiring elegant deportment was the correct placing of the head. 'The Head,' wrote Nivelon, 'being the principle Part of the human Figure, must be first considered, because it entirely governs all the Rest.' If held erect, without stiffness, the shoulders fall into proper position, the chest expands, and the back, 'straight and light', assists the 'motion

[3] John Weaver: *Anatomical and Mechanical Lectures upon Dancing*. London, 1721.

of the Hips'; they in turn affect the knees and feet. Thus 'a Person whose Head is rightly placed, is capable of Standing, Walking, Dancing, or performing any genteel Exercise in a graceful, easy and becoming Manner'[4] (Plate X*d* and *e*).

All masters impressed upon their pupils that 'in order to attain a graceful Manner of Moving, it is first necessary to know how to stand still'. Hence they turn their attention next to the placing of the feet. The feet and legs should be turned outwards to a moderate degree. 'Always turn out your feet, because that makes you stand firm, easy and graceful', is the instruction given in a little book of polite behaviour for 'Masters and Misses'. On the fly-leaf, in a large, round hand is written 'Richard Brown, Dec: 14th, 1763', and on the reverse side, 'Susanna Harford, her Book, 1771 – Sukey Harford'.[5]

Fashionable footwear again comes under censure. High heels, said Nivelon, 'cannot be easy or safe'. By straining the 'Insteps and Ancles . . . [they] prevent standing or moving' without their wearers being fearful of 'falling at every step, as is too obvious in many of the Fair Sex'.

The placing of the arms and hands is never omitted from these manuals of good deportment, and evidence that their advice was indeed the current fashion is shown in portraits and family groups of this century. The shoulders should be easy; if drawn too far back, the arms will appear 'Stiff and Lame, and the Back hollow'. To allow the arms to hang by

[4] F. Nivelon: *The Rudiments of Genteel Behaviour*. London, 1737.
[5] Anon: *The Polite Academy*. London, 1762.

PLATE XI

a. A lady, seated as described in treatises of deportment in the sixteenth century. *G. Moroni.* (*Reproduced by courtesy of the Trustees of the National Gallery, London.*)

b. A king, with similar deportment, holds counsel. Seventeenth century. *Abraham Bosse.* (*Reproduced by courtesy of the Trustees of the British Museum.*)

c. A music party in the seventeenth century. Note the popular pipe and the four-poster in the recess. A servant is washing glasses before refilling them with wine. *Artist unknown.*

d. Eighteenth-century lady seated, taking snuff. *William Hogarth.* (*Reproduced by courtesy of the Trustees of the British Museum.*)

b.

c.

d.

XI. Elegance in sitting: I

a.

b.   *c.*

XII.   Elegance in sitting: 2

the sides was considered suitable for servants but ungenteel for a gentleman. To place the hands on the hips was the attitude of certain merchants or country dancers. Men's dress, consisting of shirt, breeches, waistcoat, and coat, changed little (except for modifications of cut and trimming) throughout the century (Plates IXa, b, c, d and Xd). Evolved during the later seventeenth century, this costume was found convenient and easily adaptable to the economy of rich and poor. Pockets by now were customary in men's attire. In coat or waistcoat, the hand would feel automatically for the snuff-box, spectacle-case, or handkerchief; but the position and size of the pocket was not entirely convenient as a place in which to thrust the hands, nor was this regarded as polite except amongst close friends. In place of this, the genteel attitude adopted when in company, was to rest the right hand just inside the waistcoat (Plates Xd and XVb). This was made possible by the fashionable manner of wearing the waistcoat unbuttoned except for the three lowest buttons; the coat hung open, or was fastened by one button, below the waist. Thus, the right hand was able 'to place itself in the waistcoat, easy and genteel'. The left hand rested on the left hip, just above the sword hilt, and if the hat was removed from the head, it was placed under the left arm. In order to follow his master's detailed instructions, the pupil should place his weight upon the right foot, the left foot slightly advanced, with the knee relaxed and the foot turned a little outwards (Plate Xd).

Walking

The posture when walking was similar to that when standing; erect, relaxed, and without affectation; the steps, moderate in length, made with the heel touching the ground first. The

---

PLATE XII

a. A music party in the eighteenth century. Note the erect posture of the ladies and the deportment of the man on the right. *Phillippe Mercier. (Reproduced by courtesy of the Trustees of the British Museum.)*

b. A model of elegant deportment in 1817. *La Belle Assemblée.*

c. 'The photograph' (c. 1860). Note gloves, cane, watch chain and the manner of buttoning the jacket.

I

knee of the leg which moves forward should be straightened just before the foot touches the ground to receive the weight of the body; the whole leg, from the hip, turned slightly outward without strain or effort.

'Respect yourself as much as others,' a boy is told,[6] and walk as decently alone as if others were with you. Never whistle or sing as you walk along' (i.e. in the street) 'for these are Marks of Clownishness and Folly.' If children walked out with their parents, governess, or teacher, it was correct for them to walk in front, being careful to remain 'upright and genteel', avoiding all 'coxcomical Airs'. But if they walked with their superiors, the usual custom of giving the wall, and walking on the left-hand of the superior, had to be observed. Unless there was insufficient room to walk abreast, it was correct now for children to walk alongside the superior, rather than behind. In circumstances where they were obliged to walk behind, they were reminded to keep about two yards away, particularly if those in front happened to be ladies, to avoid treading on the trains of their 'Gowns, Sacks, or Trollopees'.[7]

Fashionable attitudes

Since the negligent behaviour, remarked upon by *The Spectator*, was a casting-off of superfluous ceremony, it was very different from the negligence of bedecked and beribboned cavaliers a century earlier. Some people affected the very opposite of polite reticence in their conversation, where 'the most coarse uncivilized Words in our Language' were openly used, particularly by 'the Coxcombs of the Town', as proof, in their opinion, of their being in the centre of current fashion.

The generation who watched this alteration in manners, felt that it reflected foreign influence upon the sober English character, which normally 'inclined rather to a certain Bashfulness of Behaviour', in contrast to the types met within town, who seemed 'not all to be the growth of [our] Island'. In apportioning blame for this new style of 'good breeding', *The Spectator* laid some upon the theatre. 'The Seat of Wit, when

---

[6] Matthew Towle: *The Young Gentleman and Lady's Private Tutor*. London, 1771.

[7] Trollopees. Any garments which trail behind.

one speaks as a Man of the Town and the World, is the Play-house. . . . The Application of Wit in the Theatre has a strong Effect upon the Manners of our Gentlemen, as the Taste of it has upon the Writings of our Authors.' While agreeing that it might appear presumptuous to 'tax the Writings of such as have long had the general Applause of a Nation', it asks whether it is necessary when supposedly portraying 'a Fine Gentleman', as in the character of Sir Foppling Flutter, that he should be made to 'Trample upon all Order and Decency'.[8]

An affectation of the period was the mis-pronunciation or misuse of words; also those who treated others as if they were deaf – the 'Loud Speakers' who always appeared to 'declare themselves', as though giving an oration. Young ladies who returned from a sojourn in France, were apt to imitate the sprightly airs and loud manners of speaking of that nation. Whereas the English child was brought up to believe that nothing 'points out ill-bred People more than talking loud in the Street', amongst the fashionable set, it appeared that 'to speak Loud in Publick Assemblies' was, in their opinion, 'looked upon as Parts of a refined Education'.[9]

Laughter

The question of laughter occurs again and again, and we find the attitude of the eighteenth-century moralist little different from that of his medieval prototype. Whilst among peoples of peasant stock, gusts of laughter rolling around the gathering were not only tolerated but expected, the polite world desired to impose restraint of behaviour. This restraint included the control of such natural actions as laughter. 'Having mentioned laughing,' Lord Chesterfield solemnly addresses his son, then aged sixteen, 'I must particularly warn you against it. . . . Frequent and loud laughter is the characteristic of folly and ill manners: it is the manner in which the mob expresses their silly joy at silly things; and they call it being merry.' While smiling was very right and proper at most times, laughter was connected with 'low buffoonery or silly accidents', and not with 'true wit or sense',

[8] *The Spectator*: No. 65 (Steele) 15 May 1711. Vol. I.
[9] *The Spectator*: No. 45 (Addison) 21 Aupril 1711. Vol. I.

the property of which was to please the mind and 'give cheerfulness to the countenance'.[10]

Tobacco

'Tobacco is very much used in England,' wrote Misson, 'the
very Women take it in abundance, particularly in the Western
Counties.' 'But why', he adds, 'the *very* Women? We wonder
that, in certain Places it should be common for Women to
take Tobacco; why should we wonder at it? The Women of
of Devonshire and Cornwall wonder that the Women of
Middlesex do *not* take Tobacco.'[11] Many such observations
noted by M. Misson on his travels in England were drawn from
the merchant classes, who probably retained a preference for
a clay pipe, as had their ancestors of the seventeenth century.
In fashionable society the taking of snuff was widespread, and
was to remain in vogue for many years. Doubtless, at this time,
it would have seemed strange to imagine that the taking of
snuff should ever disappear from the world of fashion; even as
today many consider smoking an indispensable amenity of
existence. Apart from the physical satisfaction of taking snuff
and inhaling tobacco, there is, it seems, a certain confidence
gained from the use of trifling properties which are carried on
the person. To appear at ease, the sixteenth-century gentleman
and lady learned to use gloves, pomanders, lockets, and fans.
Men and women of the seventeenth century used the snuff-box
and fan to help fill, perhaps, an awkward silence; the eighteenth-century beaux and their ladies refined the art of the
snuff-box and the fan for similar reasons unconnected with
mere physical pleasure; their modern equivalent might light
a cigarette or pipe, knowing, as they did, that such little
actions give a sense of release from tension ('However low and
poor the taking of snuff argues a man to be in his own stock
of thoughts, or means to employ his braine and his fingers').[12]
From this, as everyone knows, there develop fashionable tricks
in the handling of such trifles. Richard Steele, in his 'Exercise
of the Snuff-Box, according to the most fashionable Airs and

---

[10] Chesterfield: *Letters to his Son and Others*. Everyman.
[11] F. M. Misson (Ed.): *M. Misson's Memoirs*. Trans. Mr Ozell. London,
1719.
[12] *The Tatler*: No. 35. 'Snuff'. Everyman, Dent. London, 1953.

FIG. 8   A lady wearing a wide hoop. Eighteenth century.
H. Gravelot. Engraved by L. Truchy (*British Museum*)

Motions', offers, in mock seriousness, to teach 'Young Mer-
chants . . . the Ceremony of the Snuff-Box, or Rules for offering
Snuff to a Stranger, a Friend, or a Mistress, according to the
Degree of Familiarity or Distance'.[13] (Plate XI*d*, and Fig. 3.)

THE LADY
    For women, the eighteenth century is remembered as another
period of the hooped petticoat. Following the softly flowing
skirts of the Stuart era, the reign of William and Mary saw the

[13] *The Spectator* : No. 138. Vol. II. 'Advertisement.' Everyman. London,
1934.

introduction of a small 'bustle' with the skirts of the gown looped back, forming part of the train. About 1710 or 1711, this was superseded by the 'round hoop', an invention, said *The Tatler*, which made the petticoats of ladies too wide for entering into any coach or [*sedan*] chair' (Fig. 8). Innovations in dress are seldom adopted by the whole country as soon as they appear, and in the days when communications were slow and difficult it took longer for the latest town fashions to reach the country districts. 'A Man who takes a Journey into the Country is as much surprized as one who visits in a Gallery of old Family-Pictures.' It amused the town gentlemen to see a country beau who wore 'his own Hair when . . . at home', but when appearing at the County Sessions, was dressed up in 'a most monstrous Flaxen Periwig that was made in King William's reign'. Those who had occasion to travel some distance from the centres of fashion, told their friends that they almost fancied themselves 'in King Charles the Second's Reign, the People having made very little Variations in their Dress since that time'.

A certain lady of the manor in a country town, who had spent the winter in London, returned wearing the large hoop. Startling the congregation on a Sunday, she 'filled the Area of the Church and walked up to her Pew, with unspeakable Satisfaction, amidst the Whispers, Conjectures and Astonishment of the whole Congregation'.

The fashion was not confined to the upper classes. The country girl, with her bundle carried on her head, swayed along the lanes in her wide petticoat. But this garment, like the Spanish farthingale of the sixteenth century, could look elegant only if its wearer managed it with dexterity; an art not easy in all circumstances – particularly in a strong wind.

Walking

Walking with short, smooth steps, women had once again adopted a fashion which gave them an appearance of almost floating, as they moved amongst their pastel-shaded, satin- or silk-clad companions. In standing and walking, the head and body were held very upright; the shoulders and arms relaxed; the hands held in front at 'the Point of the Shape' (the point of the boned bodice), with the palms turned upward and a little inward toward the body; the right hand, which usually held a fan, placed over the left (Plate X*e*).

The little girl, who closely copied her mother, was told when walking to 'take short steps and do not lift up your Feet too high'. Like her mother, she wore skirts down to the ground. The advancing leg was to be placed firmly, the knee straightened just before the foot touched the ground, the foot and leg turned somewhat outward.

Sitting

The stiffly boned bodice remained in fashion. These unbending corsets caused discomfort to the wearer unless the body maintained its upright posture (Plates XI*d* and XII*a*). To recline in the privacy of one's own room while wearing loose, easeful garments was one thing; but once dressed, there was no relief; the monstrous fashion imprisoned the body with inflexible rigidity – even of those wretched ladies who fainted in the not uncommon fit of the 'vapours'. In 1742, Lady Mary Wortley Montague wrote from Avignon:[14] 'Here are several English ladies established, none I ever saw before; but they behave with decency, and give a good impression of our conduct, though their pale complexions and stiff stays do not give the French any inclination to imitate our dress.'[15]

Fans

The folding fan, by this time, had become as much a part of a lady's attire as were her head-dress or other accessories (Plates IX*e*, X*e*, and XV*b*). Indeed, so much so, that since the Restoration the manufacture of fans contributed substantially to the trade of England. 'It imploys multitudes of Men, Women and Children', claimed the manufacturers, in the use of paper, leather, silk, etc., made in the country. In addition there were 'great numbers imploy'd in Painting, Varnishing, and Japanning, and preparing abundance of Materials for Fans'; while whale-bone, tortoise-shell, ivory, box, ebony, and other woods were imported from Turkey, Russia, and the West Indies in exchange for English cloth, 'to the great advantage . . . of His

[14] Lady Mary Wortley Montagu: *Letters*. Everyman. London, 1934. p. 324. Letter of 1 June 1742.
[15] The French used much make-up.

Majesty's Customs as of the Woollen Manufacturers'.[16] The grievance of the manufacturers of fans was that the importation of Indian fans and fan-sticks would put vast numbers of poor people out of work. It is unlikely that these solemn thoughts entered the heads of the fine ladies as they toyed elegantly with this 'Weapon', as *The Spectator* named it.

The uses of a fan, as a shield from the sun or a too-hot fire, as a means of creating a cooling breeze, or to deter unwanted flies and midges, can be understood. At other times the fan was kept folded, and any unreasonable fluttering and twirling of it would appear absurd and affected. At the same time, the fan gave scope for an infinite variety of expression, particularly in the hands of a practised exponent. It was this aspect of the fan which became both a happy target for satirists of the day, and the source of fanciful interpretations of the inner meaning of the language of the fan.

A woman might possess all the airs and graces of what some persons imagined was good breeding. She could take snuff, or use her handkerchief in the most agreeable manner; laugh with the refinement of the best bred, or 'extend her little finger as appositely' as the highest in the land.[17] Yet 'all these talents will avail her nothing from the shafts of ridicule', she was warned, 'if she uses her fan in a bourgeois manner'. In fact, according to informed opinion, it was by the innumerable ways of handling a fan that 'one distinguises the Princess from the Countess, and the Marchioness from the Commoner'.

In the telling of a story, the fan would move 'to and fro like a pigeon's wing in flight – snapping shut as each sentence ends'. At the end of a gesturing arm, it added *élan* to a greeting given from the depths of a landau. And at the ball:

> Unnumbered fans to cool the crowded fair
> With breathing Zephyrs move the circling air.[18]

'What grace the Fan can convey in the hands of a Lady who knows how to use it! It weaves, it twists, it snaps shut,

---

[16] *The Fan-makers grievance* (petitions addressed to King Charles II).

[17] This, and further quotations dealing with the fan are taken (in translation) from *Le Livre de Quatre Couleurs* by L'A de Caracciolo. Paris, 1760.

[18] Soame Jenyns: *The Art of Dancing.* 1729. London, 1790.

opens, rises, falls – to suit occasion and circumstance . . . . So, too, a woman vulgarly got up, rather dull and plain, becomes supportable if she knows how to wield a Fan and guides its movements knowledgeably.'

The fan was credited, moreover, with being capable of conveying more precise meaning that mere gestures of elegance. The language of love, said the Spaniards, could be interpreted by flowers and by gestures of the fan – the second being the easier method. (See Appendix III.)

Meanwhile, the English miss was instructed in the management of her fan, being told that 'the Fan is genteel and useful, therefore it is proper that young ladies should know how to make a genteel and proper Use of it; in order that they may do so, I have pointed out to them six Positions of the Fan, genteel and very becoming.'[19]

In learning these positions – and no doubt she did so, for in the fashionable family-group paintings of this period, the fair sex are shown often with their fans in the said positions – did she know, or guess, that some bore a singular likeness to those supposedly used in flirtatious conversation?

Attention to deportment

'A Young Woman of Good Sense, will never think it beneath her Care and Study to cultivate the Graces of her outward Mien and Figure . . . for, as from the happy disposition of the Hands, Feet, and other Parts of the Body, there arises a genteel Deportment; so, where we see a young Lady standing in a genteel Position or adjusting herself properly in Walking, Dancing, or Sitting in a graceful Manner, we never fail to admire that exterior Excellence of Form . . . suited to the Rules of Decency, Modesty and good Manners'.[20]

So fashionable was the desire to behave with the decorum then accepted in society that it was hardly necessary to give this reminder. Nor was it only the families of quality who desired this accomplishment for their daughters. A young girl of a well-to-do family received regular instruction in deportment, and the visits of the dancing master, attended by his

[19] Towle: *The Young Gentleman and Lady's Private Tutor*. London, 1771.
[20] Anon: *The Polite Academy*. London, 1762.

violinist – if he, himself, did not play the instrument – were as frequent as the visits of masters of French, music and other subjects. For such as could not afford the fees for private tuition, there were the dancing schools, and also an abundance of literature which catered for their needs. A self-confessed eavesdropper who found himself at a dancing school amidst a 'Motherly Assembly of Cheapside Quality', records the conversations of one fond mother to another: 'Truly, as long as I and her Father are able to give it her, she shall want no Education to make her a Gentlewoman; for tho' we sell Ale . . . we get our Money as Honestly, and Enjoy ourselves as Comfortably as any People in our Station. . . . Marry do we. I don't know why, if we are able, we should not give our Children as good Breeding as any Body.'[21]

'Good Breeding' was the term used to indicate correct and elegant deportment of the body, and the outward show of civil behaviour, whereas 'good Manners' implied moral behaviour.

The upbringing of girls was concerned mainly with their outward deportment. Such persons as were disturbed by the general lack of education amongst women, were still struggling to present their point of view, although even they considered it was not proper to engage women 'in Studies that may turn their Brains'. Serious studies included 'Politicks, the Military Art, Law, Philosophy, and Divinity', none of which were suitable for women. 'There is nothing more neglected than the Education of Daughters', cried Fénelon, 'it is often wholly determined by Custom and the Capricios of . . . ignorant and indifferent Mothers.' But, he adds, 'there must be caution, not to make them ridiculous by making them learned'.[22] The Spectator supported this complaint with the observation that in educating girls, too much attention was paid to their exterior appearance, while with boys the emphasis was too much on the mind and too little, it seemed, on outward demeanour. Says The Spectator: A girl when 'safely brought from her Nurse . . . is delivered to the Hands of her Dancing Master; and with a Collar round her Neck, the pretty wild Thing is

[21] Anon: The Dancing School. London, 1700.
[22] F. de Salignac de la Mothe, Viscount Fénelon: Instructions for the Education of a Daughter. Englished by G. Hicks. London, 1707.

taught a fantastical Gravity of Behaviour'. The true art of education was 'To make the Mind and Body improve together . . . to make Gesture follow Thought, and not let Thought be employed upon Gesture'.[23]

Customs tend to change imperceptibly. From the sixteenth century, polite ceremony followed the usage of kissing one's own hand when giving or receiving an object. As we have seen, this gesture was made by bringing the hand towards the mouth, not quite touching it, before extending the arm. Gestures of this nature are apt to become curtailed with the passing of time, for example, a mere circular motion of the hand and arm as it is extended forward. This is exactly what we find described in English treatises of the eighteenth century, in which the kissing of the hand is no longer mentioned.

Before presenting his gift, or whatever it was, a boy was told to remove his hat, and put it under the left arm; the arm hanging straight down over the hat, as it remained in position, without undue pressure. The right hand and arm were then raised forward, curving the arm by bending the elbow and wrist; on giving the object, the whole arm was extended, thereby making a circular gesture outwards towards the person before him; at the same time the right leg was moved forward in order to make the forward bow (see Appendix I(f)iii) (Plates IXc and XVb). The girl began her presentation by making a curtsy; holding her hands in the correct position (see *Walking*, p. 134), and being careful neither to approach the person too closely, nor to stay so far off that they were obliged to move towards her. On rising from the curtsy, she presented her gift, making the same gesture as that described for the boy. She was then told: 'When you have given, or received, it, withdraw your Hand gently in a circular Manner. Place it upon the other hand; then you will be in the Posture for Curtseying. Making your Curtsey exactly as we have described before. If you leave the Room . . . walk gently away. When you come to the Door, turn and make another Curtsey.'[24]

It is easy to see how this rather meaningless gesture, in time, would fade away, to become entirely forgotten.

[23] *The Spectator*: No. 66 (Steele) 15 May 1711. Vol. 1.
[24] Anon: *The Polite Academy*. London, 1762.

(b) SALUTATIONS

With the arrival of the eighteenth century it might almost seem as though the labour expended by previous generations towards forming the wholly poised gentleman and lady, had now matured. This attitude may be sensed in the numerous works concerned with the rules of polite behaviour, the art of dancing and of genteel deportment, which appeared during this period, in this century all these books began to speak, as it were, with the same voice.

In England, French fashions and manners remained greatly in vogue, and the instructions given by the English authors of courtesy books faithfully followed their French masters.

The art of making a graceful bow no longer depended upon flowing gestures and deep obeisances. Rather it was an art which concealed art, for every action of the well-bred gentleman now expressed something of that refined reserve which for generations to come was to be the hallmark of polite society. Every movement, as in a bow, was well-considered, exact, and without superfluity of gesture. Even the manner of taking off or replacing the hat, followed prescribed and carefully timed movements.

The Hat

The gradual uniformity of fashion had by now instituted a single style, that of the three-cornered hat, amongst men of almost all classes and ages (Plate IX). This style of wearing the wide brim buttoned up to form three points, was used on all occasions, except possibly in the rain, when it could be unbuttoned to give protection to the wearer. It was placed with care on top of a curled wig, with one of the three points over the left eye, rather than the centre of the forehead. In the presence of company, at least, it still remained a part of men's attire indoors, as well as out, and the knowledge of how to remove or replace it, or hold it when not on the head, with ease and grace, was therefore taught at an early age to boys from whom a 'polite address' would be expected.

'Be indebted to no man for a Hat, tho' he be far inferior to you; but discreetly pay him home his Salute.' So advised Adam

Petrie in 1719[25] and, although both his style and his matter by then appeared old-fashioned, an acquaintance is said to have confirmed that Petrie behaved in exact agreement with the *Rules* he laid down. 'A very necessary matter for everyone, whatever their station, to be informed upon, is the correct manner of raising one's hat and making a graceful bow', wrote Pierre Rameau, the French dancing master in 1725.[26] Thereupon he gives most detailed observations concerning the manner of taking off the hat (Plate IX*a* and *b*).

The Bow

If the bow was to be made approaching someone in a room, or elsewhere, a boy was told: 'Take off your Hat in the manner just directed, and bring it down to your Knee' (Plate IX*b*). 'Let the Inside of the Hat front the Person you bow to, and let your Hand fall straight down; which Posture shows an Arm handsomely.' Displaying the inside of the hat, rather than concealing it against the body as in former times, came into fashion with the wearing of wigs; the supposition being that the inside no longer became soiled and, being the fashion, it would be the practice for all to conform, whether or not a young boy wore a wig.

In the ordinary bow the hand which raised the hat from the head was brought straight down to the side of the body, whereas for the 'passing bow' it was sufficient merely to raise the hat off the head. If, however, the persons were promenading in some fashionable place, such as the Tuileries in Paris, it was customary to carry the hat under the left arm, and in this case before making a passing bow the hat was taken from under the arm with the right hand and held low, near the body, before bowing.

'The Bow, being a token of respect and esteem, must be made according to the quality of the persons whom one salutes, and to the particular consideration inspired by merit and character. . . . It is the usual custom to make a bow on entering a room, on leaving it, on meeting someone, before beginning a dance, and on finishing it. The best masters teach the

[25] Adam Petrie: *Rules of Good Deportment, or of Good Breeding.* Edinburgh, 1719.
[26] P. Rameau: *Le Maître à Danser.* 1725. Trans. C. W. Beaumont. London, 1931.

manner of making these reverences in detail, and knowledge of high society, and of all true civility, requires its proper application.'[27]

In the eighteenth century, bows were made in three ways; those made when greeting or leaving (Appendix I(f)iii and iv), and that made in passing (I(f) ii). The contemporary passion of analysing everything in the greatest detail caused dancing masters of the century to claim anything from two to five types of bows.

The Curtsy

Apart from a few technical details, curtsies of this century are the same as those of the seventeenth century. Once again there are two types – the passing curtsy and the more respectful one. (Appendix I(f) vi and vii.)

(c) HOSTS AND GUESTS

The fashion of paying and receiving visits altered little from that of the previous century. Gradually, in place of the stiff formality of courtesy visits to grand personages, these gatherings began to develop into the more informal friendliness of social intercourse. Visits of ceremony were still customary on occasions of marriage, birth, or mourning. At other times, visiting amongst 'persons of the first quality' was as popular in England as in France, but in England this form of social entertainment was not used by 'the Ordinary Sort of People', as was the custom among French shopkeepers. There, the wives, donning a trailing gown, participated in rounds of tedious visits, often merely sitting dumbly, with folded arms, contributing nothing of worth to anyone. In England, where people visited one another in the evenings, they came 'to see one another with their Work in their Hands and Cheerfulness in their Countenance, without Rule or Constraint'. The art of conversation was a pleasure enjoyed by those who had the knowledge and wit to contribute to these gatherings.

Ladies receive visits while in bed or when dressing
The fashion amongst ladies of quality of receiving their

[27] Anon: *L'Art de la Danse*. Paris, 1745.

visitors while in bed in the morning, or finishing their toilet, was considered smart by the modish set, who indulged in the latest fancies of what they regarded as good breeding. How artfully could a woman give herself an air of wise deliberation by a studious contemplation of a pin-cushion, or the ivory comb with which she combed her flowing hair. How non-chalantly at ease could she appear as she gained a moment's pause by applying her tongue to a patch, which required to be placed with nice judgement in exactly the right spot. Visiting day was a serious occupation to the fashionable lady, attracting the attention of contemporary satirists.

The tea-table

In England, the habit of taking tea introduced all classes to a new diversion in the solemn interchange of visits. The drink was used by people of quality on the Continent long before it became fashionable in England, where it began to be taken more widely about the middle of the seventeenth century. By the eighteenth, it was firmly established as a favourite drink of the nation. At first, it was regarded as an evil to be fought against – 'pernicious to health, obstructing industry, and impoverishing the nation'. The tittle-tattle of 'tea-table talk' incurred some censure amongst the older-fashioned of the upper classes, although the beverage was considered less harmful in these circles than for the working man. But fashion seldom troubles with gloomy predictions, and the popularity of the tea habit in this period was a favourite subject of contemporary portrait painters in their elegant conversation pieces of the tea-table. Here one sees the imbibers, served by black pages, Indian servants, or members of the family, seated very upright with handle-less cups poised delicately in their fingers. As for 'tea-table talk', it has remained much the same throughout the ages – particularly among women, for tea was a great beverage for women. 'I was lately at a Tea-Table,' writes Steele in *The Spectator* in 1712, 'where some young Ladies entertained the Company with a relation of a Coquet in the Nenghbourhood . . . the Discourse, which from being witty, grew to be malicious. . . .'[28] *The Spectator* found

[28] *The Spectator*: No. 392 (Steele) 30 May 1712. Vol. V. Everyman.

much to comment upon in the habit of taking tea, and was the recipient of letters upon the subject. One distressed aunt in 1714, found her nieces altogether unmanageable with their preoccupation over 'their Dress, their Tea, and their Visits'. This lady complained that the art of needlework had become quite neglected. Whereas she had spent hours quilting petticoats, embroidering covers for beds, chairs, and hangings for more than fifty years, her nieces now spent their days thinking of nothing but dress, plays, and visits: 'It grieves my Heart to see a couple of proud idle Flirts sipping their Tea, for a whole Afternoon, in a Room hung round with the Industry of their great Grandmother.'[29]

Excessive formality unfashionable

In all periods there will be contradictions concerning modes of current behaviour. Much depends upon the view or experience of the observer. Nameless small points of etiquette change imperceptibly with the fashions favoured by a particular set of people. Only those outside the set, or whose perception enables them to place themselves outside, become aware of the changes. The eighteenth-century tendency to break away from burdensome formality was initiated – as many such movements are – by the ranks of society who felt secure in position or birth. They found it easier to disregard the petty tyrannies of artificial formality, than did those who might fear that their attitude would be misconstrued as ignorance of correct behaviour. *The Spectator* decries the wearisome politeness of old-fashioned or country folk. 'This Rural Politeness is very troublesome to a Man of my Temper, who

[29] ibid., No. 606. 13 October 1714. Vol. VIII.

PLATE XIII

a. Sixteenth century. The Countess of Leicester and her children. The boy in petticoats with sword. *M. Gheeraerts the elder.* (*Reproduced by permission of the Rt. Hon. Viscount De L'Isle, from his collection at Penshurst Place, Kent.*)

b. Eighteenth century. The Graham children. *William Hogarth.* (*Reproduced by courtesy of the Trustees of the Tate Gallery, London.*)

a.

b.

XIII.   Children—small replicas of their elders

a.

b.

XIV. Contrasts

generally take the Chair that is next me, and walk first or last, in Front or in the Rear, as Chance directs.' Not so these country gentlefolk who, in their anxiety not to be thought unmannerly, became tedious in their ostentatious observation of etiquette. Even, continued *The Spectator*, 'Honest Will Wimble, who I should have thought had been altogether un-infected with Ceremony, gives me an abundance of Trouble in this Particular. . . . When we are going out of the Hall, he runs behind me, and last Night, as we were walking in the Fields, stopped short at a Stile till I came up to it, and upon my making Signs to him to get over, told me, with a serious Smile, that sure I believed they had no Manners in the Country'.[30]

Generally speaking, a bow or curtsy was directed to an individual by way of greeting, leave-taking, or in acknowledge-ment of some courtesy (Plate XV*b*), although these could be made to the company as a whole, on entering a room where a number of people were assembled. These courtesies were the normal practice, though there must have been many, like Lady Mary Wortley Montagu, who found the formality tedious and absurd. 'I won't trouble you', she wrote to Mr Pope, 'with farewell compliments, which I think generally as impertinent as curtseys at leaving the room, when the visit has been too long already.'[31]

Persons in attendance on those of high rank were not saluted, unless permission was first requested from the superior.

[30] ibid., No. 119. 17 July 1711. Vol. II.
[31] *Letters*. Everyman. p. 67. Letters of 14 Sept. 1716.

PLATE XIV

a. A christening feast in a humble home in the seventeenth century. Note the swaddled infant. The boys keep their hats off, and the wine-glass is held by the base in the fashion of the day. *Louis le Nain.* (*Reproduced by courtesy of the Musée du Louvre.*)

b. A winter party in a rich house, same period. Note the four-poster, the napkins being placed on the table-cloth; the up-holstered chairs, the windows with shutters but no curtains. The small girl has her robe tucked up. *Abraham Bosse.* (*Reproduced by courtesy of the Trustees of the British Museum.*)

K

Royalty

No one, not even those of high rank, who accompanied a sovereign, would receive a salute when in the presence of a member of the royal family; nor was it correct to make a bow or curtsy to a royal person, unless in recognition of some word or look. At an initial encounter with royalty, a reverence (bow or curtsy) was made when speaking with, or serving, them.

On an occasion when King George III had been talking to Fanny Burney about her novel, *Evelina*, the Queen entered. 'Immediately seeing the King, she made him a low curtsy, and cried: "Oh, your Majesty is here!"' Fanny Burney, who was standing by, was conscious that the Queen had noticed, and had curtsied to, her. Owing, however, to her being 'too near-sighted' to be sure that the curtsy was intended for her, she felt in a predicament. 'I was hardly ever in a situation more embarrassing; I dared not return what I was not certain I had received.' The King came to her rescue by mentioning Miss Burney's name to Her Majesty, whereupon Fanny was able to drop a curtsy immediately. At another time the King and Queen, who had been visiting Mrs Delany, rose to go. 'Mrs Delany,' writes Miss Burney, 'put on her Majesty's cloak, and she [the Queen] took a very kind leave of her. She then curtsied separately to us all, and the King handed her to the carriage. It is the custom for everybody they speak to, to attend them out, but they would not suffer Mrs Delany[32] to move.' 'I never go from her [the Queen's] presence till I am dismissed; no one does, not even when they come in only with a hurried message – except the pages, who enter merely as messengers. . . . The general form of the dismission . . . is in these words: "Now I will let you go", which the Queen manages to speak with a grace that takes from them all air of authority.' This, says Miss Burney, was a mark of honour, used to people of the first rank, even the Princesses. Pages and wardrobe women who came only for the purpose of some ordinary duty, left after the work was done without conversing more than was necessary.[33]

[32] Then aged about eighty-five years.
[33] Fanny Burney: *Diary*. Everyman, Dent. London, 1950. pp. 105, 108, and 126.

Managing the train of a gown

Fanny Burney also speaks of the fatigue of standing for a long time when attending their majesties on formal occasions, and of the difficulty of walking backwards in a dress with a long train. Lady Charlotte Bertie, who had a sprained ankle, found herself obliged to walk backwards from the king's presence: 'Back she went, perfectly upright, without one stumble, without ever looking once behind to see what she might encounter, and with as graceful a motion, and as easy an air, as I ever saw anybody enter a long room, she retreated, I am sure, full twenty yards backwards out of one.' Lady Charlotte performed this down the centre of the room, whereas Fanny made her exit near the wainscot, taking a few steps, then pretending to examine some portrait while disengaging her train from the heels of her shoes, until at last she escaped.[34]

MANNERS OF CHILDREN

The teaching of manners begins always with children, and with them the rules of behaviour were still strictly adhered to when in company. This formal conduct was practised first by them towards their parents, as in medieval days. Because children of the well-to-do were attended and supervised by nurses, tutors, or governesses, parents were beings who stood aloof, to be treated with a formality of behaviour undreamed of by their descendants today.

At all times, children had to bow or curtsy on their first daily encounter with their parents, or with any other adult; similarly, whenever they entered or left a room where there was any company – parents or others. 'Let this be your constant Rule and by these means you will find this kind of Behaviour will become familiar and easy to you', was the advice commonly given; nor was this idea new, neither was it applied to western behaviour alone. (See Appendix I(f) v.)

Descending downstairs to breakfast, they bid their parents good-morning with a bow or curtsy. 'After you have bowed to them, enquire after their Health, as "How-do you do, Sir, or Papa, I hope you had a good Night's repose?"' A similar question was put to 'Mamma', or 'Madam'. 'Thus, having

[34] ibid., pp. 141–2.

genteely asked your Parents how they do . . . then will your
Papa or Mamma bid you sit down, if they think proper.'³
Having finished breakfast, they were to rise, give their parents
thanks for their good breakfast, and leave the room. Not much
had changed in two centuries!

Tutors, governesses, servants

After the parents, the members of the household with whom
the children were most concerned were their tutors and
governesses. Their behaviour to these was as punctilious as to
their parents. 'Whenever your Master or Governess speaks to
you, it is your Duty to get up and bow or curtsy to them, and
to stand still till such times it is their Pleasure to bid you sit
down; then bow or curtsy and sit down.'³⁵ Towards the
servants of the household, children were taught to behave
with courtesy; asking them politely to do a service, and thanking them when done.

Children on a visit

When taken to visit a friend's house, children learned that
it was their place to receive graciously the hospitality and
attention shown them by their hosts, whilst being careful to
avoid causing more trouble than necessary. By observing the
correct degree of deportment and ceremony, they would appear
sensible and well-bred, but with that 'Ease and Freedom' which
constituted 'real Politeness'. This meant that children should
acquire the habit of making these actions and words *appear*
natural and graceful. Much was consistent with common
politeness, based on consideration for others, which is taken
for granted by most people today.

The Hat

When entering a room, they were to stand aside, to let
others go in first. A boy of the eighteenth century wore his hat
indoors, as was the custom of the period, but before entering
a room, he had to remember to take it off. Having entered, he
made his first bow to the mistress of the house, then to the
master. Should neither of these be present, he bowed to the

³⁵ Towle: *The Young Gentleman and Lady's Private Tutor.* London.
1771.

assembled company (Fig. 9), unless he was told to seek out the lady of greatest importance. This lady might be one of highest rank, or 'the oldest in the Room'. Should the boy be unable to distinguish her from the rest, he would be sure to find her at the 'upper' end of the room, where such persons sat. A small girl presented herself with the same formality, dropping her curtsies with practised care.

FIG. 9   A bow made to the company on entering a room. Eighteenth century. *Phillippe Mercier (British Museum)*

Behaviour in company

Whether a child was a visitor in another house, or was introduced to company in his or her own home, the behaviour was the same. On finding that their parents were entertaining friends, children asked a servant to tell their parents that they were outside, for they did not enter the room without being bidden. First making their bow or curtsy, they asked their parents what they wished. If allowed to remain, they went to the 'lowest' end of the room; never were they to 'crowd the Fire'. They had to sit upright, without stretching out the legs, swinging them, or lolling. The correct posture for the boy was that in imitation of his father; one hand inside the waistcoat, the other on his knees, his hat under his arm. The girl held her hands, or perhaps a fan, in her lap (see Appendix III). They

FIG. 10   A man seated, showing the hat and the sword.
Eighteenth century. *H. Gravelot*. (*British Museum*)

were never to speak, unless first spoken to; never to stare at
people. To 'sing or whistle in Company', they were reminded,
were 'idle Tricks of vulgar Children'. Too much coughing,
sneezing, and blowing the nose was not polite; as for hawking
and spitting, these were now regarded as obnoxious habits.

Taking leave

When the family rose to take leave of their hosts, the children left the room after their elders, being careful to remember

their obeisances to the company. At the outer door of the house, they bowed or curtsied to the lady or gentleman who had accompanied the family thus far – 'for you may depend upon it, they are very genteel people who wait on their Guests to the Door'.

Children of more advanced years

As childhood was left behind, this strictness of behaviour was somewhat relaxed. 'In the first place,' those of more advanced years were told, 'you are excused from getting up when you speak, as all younger Gentlemen and Ladies do.' To tutors, governesses, and elderly people who entered a room where they were seated, they would rise if a question or remark was addressed to them.

CHAPTER VI

The Nineteenth Century

(*a*) DEPORTMENT AND ETIQUETTE

THE GENTLEMAN

The precepts given by Lord Chesterfield continued to form the basis of many works concerning good manners during the early years of the nineteenth century. In his note to *The New Chesterfield* (1830), the editor states that he 'could not do the rising generation a greater service than by collecting these valuable precepts . . . digesting them under distinct heads [into] a system of the most useful instruction'.

This manual, addressed to ladies as well as to men, reflects the altered outlook of the new society. Compared with previous centuries, the nineteenth century was not so much a 'mannered' period, as one where good or bad taste counted for a great deal. Ostentation in any form was shunned by the polite world; to be thought vulgar was to become an outcast from this world.

The zenith of mannered artificiality was reached towards the end of the seventeenth century; thereafter a gentle descent took place, toward a less obvious display of outward show. From now on, each succeeding generation stressed that all well-bred contemporary behaviour had become less rigidly formal than that of their forbears. 'The manner, in short, which a man must aspire to, is one which will give ease, and not embarrassment, to others. . . . What applies to manner may be transferred in most respects to that bearing which distinguishes a man in society. But the times change much in this respect, and the old courteous dignity with which the beaux of my younger days behaved, has given way to greater ease, and sometimes I fear, to too great freedom. I do not know whether to regret, or not, the strict courteousness of those times. It often amounted to affectation; it was not natural to be ever bowing low, making set speeches, raising a lady's hands to one's lips, or pressing one's own upon the region of the heart, but at the same time I regret the lounging familiarity which we see too prevalent among young men of the present day.'[1]

Thomas Tegg in 1838, borrows much from Chesterfield, but directs his advice to young people in a different stratum of society from that of Philip Stanhope. 'Next to good breeding,' he says, 'is a genteel manner and gentlemanly carriage, wholly free from those ill habits, and awkward actions to which, nevertheless, many very worthy and superior persons are addicted.' Awkwardness of behaviour, he continues, while having 'nothing in it criminal . . . is such an offence to good manners and good breeding, that it is universally despised'.[2]

It was recognized that good bodily carriage should be acquired in childhood and youth, in order to form a good habit; the means of obtaining this was by exercise, gymnastics, and the like. Dignity was regarded as an indispensable asset, and this could never be acquired by a slouching gait. The other extreme, of 'curving the back inwards', in an exaggerated posture of uprightness, with the chest thrust out so as to make 'a presence', was equally ridiculous. 'Avoid stiffness on the one hand, lounging on the other. Be natural and perfectly at your ease, whether in walking or sitting, and aspire to calm confidence rather than loftiness.'

The acquisition of a 'calm confidence', inculcated from childhood, could only have the effect of making the English appear aloof and stand-offish to strangers. Emerson's observations on the behaviour of the English in 1833 and 1847, as they appeared to him, reveal the behaviour which educated persons in this country had grown to regard as good manners. He saw in the English an 'incuriosity, and stony neglect, each of every other. Each man walks, eats, drinks, shaves, dresses, gesticulates, and, in every manner, acts and suffers without

[1] Anon: *The Habits of Good Society*. London, *c*. 1860. pp. 248–9.
[2] Thomas Tegg: *A Present for an Apprentice*. 1838. 2nd ed., London, 1848.

reference to the bystanders, in his own fashion, only careful not to interfere with them, or annoy them'. No one seemed concerned with the personal eccentricity of others, so that, if 'an Englishman walks in a pouring rain, swinging his closed umbrella like a walking stick; wears a wig, or a shawl, or a saddle, or stands on his head . . . no remark is made. And as he has been doing this for several generations, it is now in the blood. In short, every one of these islanders is an island himself, safe, tranquil, incommunicable'.[3]

Fashionable attitudes

The fashionable world divided the day into clearly defined periods, for each of which it was necessary to wear the appropriate dress. This required consideration, for no one would be averse to receiving the current compliment – 'He always dresses as a gentleman', though what was implied by this phrase was as hard to define as were the manners of a gentleman. The same desire for unobtrusive appearance inspired both – dress and manners. It was said that showy and costly dress was worn in the days when kings were the arbiters of fashion; the influence of philosophers led to slovenly and untidy dress, and when, as in the nineteenth century, fashion was dictated 'by private gentlemen and ladies, it is often absurd and in bad taste, but generally tends towards simplicity'.

From this period onwards the essential features of men's dress changed but little. The graceful curl of a hat-brim, or a collar, might be superseded by a mode that was less uncomfortable for the wearer; tight waistcoats and even tighter breeches might give way to those which allowed greater freedom of movement. Those who were old-fashioned in their garb were derided no longer – so long as their years matched their dress. Pocket-sized volumes on etiquette and advice on dress had a ready sale judging by the numerous publications of these works. A typical observation in one of these is that 'the nearest English words for the completed toilette of a gentlemen are – harmony and becomingness; nothing must deserve the modern slang expression of "loud" '.[4] The choice

[3] R. W. Emerson: *English Traits*. (VI. 'Manners') Everyman. London, 1951, p. 52.
[4] Welden: *Etiquette for Gentlemen*. London, c. 1860.

of a man's morning attire depended on whether he dressed for the promenade in town; whether he would be in the country or by the sea, or perhaps 'touring' or shooting; all of which required the appropriate dress.

Morning attire for the promenade consisted usually of a dark-coloured frock-coat, double or single breasted; dark trousers for winter, grey or fawn in better weather. The waistcoat was of a patterned material, light or dark. A man's accessories were important: unsoiled gloves, handkerchief, and clean boots; a spotless white lining to his hat, since the inside of the hat became visible when removed from the head on making a bow; finally, the cane, or, in bad weather, an umbrella. The advantage of the last two items was that they gave some employment for his hands, for, it was said, 'the Englishman does not gesticulate when talking and in consequence has nothing to do with his hands. To put them in his pocket is the natural action, but this gives an appearance of lounging *insouciance*'. The best substitutes, therefore, were the cane or umbrella, *not* 'a parasol, unless it be given to you by a lady to carry'.[5] The nineteenth-century gentleman never used scent as was the habit of fashionable fops of earlier periods. Scent now became a prerogative of the ladies.

Standing, walking, sitting

Rules for standing, walking, and sitting, in comparison with earlier ages, were simple and brief. To stand with both legs straight or possibly with one slightly relaxed at the knee, is natural and needs little comment. In walking, the leg should be moved easily and firmly from the hip, without swaying or rocking the body. It was thought elegant to turn the feet and legs out somewhat, but only 'very little indeed'.

Throughout the years, books of good conduct echoed Della Casa's observation that it was quite unsuitable for gentlemen to be seen hurrying along the street. In the eighteen-thirties the attitude was still the same. 'Walking fast in the streets is a mark of vulgarity, implying hurry of business; it may appear well in a mechanic or tradesman, but ill suits the character of a gentleman, or a man of fashion.' Thomas Tegg asserts that

[5] Anon: *The Habits of Good Society*. London, *c.* 1860. p. 147.

to be in a hurry is the 'mark of little minds'; it is 'a proof that the business we embark on is too much for us. . . . A man of sense may be in "haste" but he is never in a "hurry" '.

'It is painful to see the want of ease with which some men sit on the edge of a chair.' These are the words of Lord Chesterfield quoted in the mid-nineteenth century. In his day, deportment commended in the sixteenth century would be considered absurdly stiff. In the nineteenth century, however, the complaint was not against too much rigidity, but against too much lounging; 'The manner in which others throw themselves back and stretch forward their legs savours too much of familiarity. You may cross your legs if you like, but not hug your knees or your toes. Straddling a chair, and tilting it up may be pardonable in a bachelor's room, but not in a lady's drawing-room.'[6]

Smoking

The habit of smoking had become firmly established. Cigar-smoking was not practised in northern Europe until the last quarter of the eighteenth century. Cigarettes were originally hand-made by the smoker himself, and even in the first years of the twentieth century, hand-made cigarettes were considered superior to the machine-made variety, the latter having only now become a flourishing manufacture.

In the nineteenth century, the unwritten law on when and where it was permissible to smoke, were enough to check the indulgence to some extent. 'One must never smoke, nor even ask to smoke, in the company of the fair.' Ladies who realized that a man wished to smoke a cigar, might tactfully ask him into the garden (in summer) to smoke it there. It was not proper to smoke in 'a room inhabited by ladies' – even one's wife or sisters. In the streets a pipe should never be smoked, nor was it in good taste to smoke at all in the streets – 'in daylight'. In any public places, especially where ladies were, or might be, smoking was not permitted; for example, at a flower-show, a promenade, a theatre, on a race-course, nor – it was hardly necessary to add – in church. 'The *tobacco-smoker in public* is the most selfish animal imaginable; he

[6] ibid., p. 251.

perseveres in contaminating the pure and fragrant air, careless whom he annoys, and is but the fitting inmate of a tavern',
cried Thomas Tegg, adding that 'smoking in the streets, or in
a theatre is only practised by shop-boys, pseudo-fashionables,
and the "swell-mob".'

In a railway carriage, it was permissible to smoke after
obtaining 'the consent of everyone present' – but never if
ladies were among the occupants. It was not correct to smoke
at all in the coffee-room of a hotel; nor, without consent, in
the presence of a clergyman. A cigar was on no account to be
offered to any churchman 'over the rank of curate'.

Those who wished to smoke, or be in the company of
smokers, if afterwards they were to meet ladies, were expected
to change their clothes – or rather their coat – to avoid offend-
ing by the smell of stale tobacco. 'A host who asks you to
smoke, will generally offer you an old coat for the purpose'. In addition, the mouth was to be rinsed and the teeth
cleaned.

THE LADY

In contrast with men's fashions, which by now had arrived
at some orthodoxy in style, women's dress presented a state
of perpetual change throughout the century. This is revealed
by the regular appearance of fashion plates, together with
descriptions of the latest trends from Paris and London. The
newest vogues displayed at Longchamps received a welcome
press in women's magazines.

The reason for this constant change seems somewhat obscure,
although the increasing wealth of society probably had much
to do with it. The conspicuous attitude of the period seems
one of eagerness to conform to whatever was regarded as
'correct'. While a particular style was in vogue – whether it
was high-waisted and clinging, the crinoline, bustle, or leg-
of-mutton sleeve – women all contrived to look singularly
alike.

The desire, manifested during the eighteenth century, to
escape from a too great formality and artificiality of behaviour,
appears also to be reflected in the greater simplicity of dress
for women and men. Introduced during the last years of the
eighteenth century – between 1795 and 1799 – these styles

continued in favour for the first quarter of the next century. Indeed, so formless were women's fashions, that they appeared as though in *négligé*. Manners and dress obviously reflect contemporary thought and circumstance. The sole effect of costume upon physical deportment is in restriction of freedom of movement. To this extent it has some bearing upon the present subject, but is not the most important factor.

The effect of better education for women was slowly altering their outlook. No longer were women expected to act the part of brainless playthings, forever chasing the whims of the moment. Instead, the young girl was taught that duty and example were her main guides; duty in doing good, and example by exhibiting good taste in her behaviour and her appearance. In place of flamboyant fashions, the newest modes were presented as being suitable, becoming, or in good taste. 'Mental improvement should always be made conducive to moral advancement: to render a young woman wise and good, to prepare her mind for the duties and trials of life, is the great purpose of education. Accomplishments, however desirable and attractive, must always be considered as secondary objects, when compared with those virtues which form the character, and influence the power of women in society.'[7] This extract is a typical example of the advice tendered to young ladies in contemporary literature for women.

With the abandonment of hooped petticoats and painted faces which were in vogue during the eighteenth century, there was a trend towards a more unaffected simplicity of manner. Nature, rather than Art, was to be the young lady's guide. The key to women's whole behaviour and deportment was 'gentleness'. The advice that ladies should avoid stiffness whether in standing, walking, or sitting, shows the reversal of the practice of the previous era, when the rigidly upright posture was the normal attitude induced by custom and costume. This extreme rigidity was admired no longer. 'In regard to the physical carriage of women, the graces of an upright form, of elegant and gentle movements, and of the desirable medium between stiffness and lounging, are desirable both for married and single. The same rules and recommenda-

---

[7] Anon: *The Young Lady's Book*. London, 1829. p. 23.

tions are applicable to both. Control over the countenance is a part of manners.'[8]

Marriage, with its responsibilities of household management, was assumed to require an added dignity of manner in women. A married woman should never appear in the least degree flirtatious. 'The bearing of married women,' it was said, 'should so far differ from that of the unmarried, that there should be greater quietness and dignity.'

Gymnastics, so long used as a training for men and boys, was creeping – in a gentle form – into the physical education of women. Indian clubs and 'chest expanders' exercised the torso and arms, while exercises for dancing gave suppleness and control to the legs and feet. To a great extent, dancing teachers had lost their long-established status in the teaching of manners and deportment. The dancing lesson no longer began with instruction on how to make a bow or a curtsy; how to enter or leave a room. Moreover, the 'practice adopted by many parents and heads of seminaries' of employing 'soldiers to teach young ladies how to walk', was criticized in *The Young Lady's Book*: 'The stiffness acquired under regimental tuition, is adverse to all the principles of grace, and annihilates the buoyant lightness which is so conducive to ease and elegance in the young.'

At all times the well-brought-up lady must try to appear as though impervious to the unbecoming effects of unusual exertion, causing her to breathe hard; or of heat and cold – making her appear either 'very hot or very blue and shivery'; in fact anything 'that detracts from the pleasure of society is in bad taste'.

Sitting

From the introduction of the long, stiffly-boned bodice in Elizabethan times, up to the later years of the eighteenth century, fashion had decreed that women should maintain an exceedingly erect posture when seated. The advice now offered was to 'avoid sitting stiffly, as if a ramrod were introduced within the dress behind'. On the other hand, lolling in the chair was not condoned. When going to sit down in the

[8] *The Habits of Good Society.* p. 272.

presence of others, a lady ought to 'sink gently into a chair, and, on formal occasions, retain her upright position; neither lounge nor sit timorously on the edge of her seat. Her feet should scarcely be shown, and not crossed'[9] (Plate XIIb).

Walking

The manner of walking well still received a good deal of attention. In the opinion of contemporary writers it was 'a point too much neglected'. Whether a lady was 'in the drawing-room, the ballroom, or during the promenade, an elegant deportment is, and ever will be, appreciated'. The steps were to be short – 'not to exceed the length of a foot'; the advancing leg should not be stiff, and there should be no effort to turn the foot out, as it will tend to throw the body awry, and give the person an appearance of being a professional dancer' (Plate Xf). The distinction between the style of dancing upon the stage and in the ballroom was clearly marked, though the steps used in the latter were based upon the same technique. With the head erect, and chest expanded, the natural motion of the body in walking, where the arms move in 'the opposition motion to the legs', was now regarded as right and proper to good walking.

Although the dancing master did not command the same importance as in earlier centuries, the benefit of being taught elegant posture and grace of movement by a good master – for those not endowed with it by nature – was considered the best method of eradicating 'faults of posture and unbecoming movement'. 'A lady may be known by her walk,' it was said; 'the short rapid steps, the shaking the body from side to side,

[9] ibid., p. 273.

PLATE XV

a. Seventeenth century. Gallants and their ladies shopping. (*Abraham Bosse.*)

b. Eighteenth century. Fashionable conversation in the London Pantheon. Note the sword of the man seated on the right (*Richard Earlom.*)

(*Reproduced by courtesy of the Trustees of the British Museum.*)

a.

b.

XV. The characteristic style of seventeenth- and
eighteenth-century deportment

a.

b.

c.

d.

e.

f.

XVI. Oddments of apparel

or the *very* slow gait which many ladies consider genteel, are equally to be deprecated.'

The promenade

Ladies, also, had their appropriate dress for walking, riding in a carriage, morning visits, as well as for balls and other social functions. English men and women who constituted the polite world of this period, had sufficient leisure to enjoy the promenade – a pastime which had retained its popularity from the days of the Stuarts. In order to see, and be seen by, the 'best people', promenaders repaired to wherever the world of current fashion happened to gather. In Stuart times it would be the Royal Exchange (transepts of old St. Pauls), or the Mall, still fashionable in Georgian England. This now gave place to the attraction of Rotten Row. If the fashionable throng was at one of the well-known watering places, the gaily dressed crowd could be seen strolling in the summer sunshine along the promenade or parade.

Towards the end of the eighteenth century, and during the nineteenth, a gentleman who walked with a lady offered her his arm. It was fashionable no longer to lead her by the hand.

PLATE XVI

a. A hinged pomander of the fifteenth century with one section open. Each section could contain a different scent. (*Victoria and Albert Museum. Crown Copyright.*)

b. Some eighteenth-century pomanders. (*Victoria and Albert Museum. Crown Copyright.*)

c. Eighteenth-century shoe and pantofle. (*Victoria and Albert Museum. Crown Copyright.*)

d. Detail from a portrait of a young woman of the seventeenth century, showing the girdle chain on which pomanders and other things were hung, fringed gauntlets and rings worn on the index fingers. *Cornelius de Vos.* (*Reproduced by permission of James Christie, Esq.*)

e. Pantofle. Green velvet with gold lace. (*Victoria and Albert Museum. Crown Copyright.*)

f. A high chopine of the seventeenth century. (*Victoria and Albert Museum. Crown Copyright.*)

L

The cut.

The widening circle of people whose newly gained wealth admitted them to a social stratum above that from which they had risen, was one of the results brought about by the Industrial Revolution. An outcome of this social upheaval was the appearance of a marked display of snobbishness, which invaded even the nursery and literature for children. A visible and unpleasant form of nineteenth-century snobbishess was the widely accepted use of the 'cut'. 'In modern civilized life as it is,' we read, 'the cut is a great institution.' Though this behaviour was used in what was termed 'good' society, the practice was condemned as pretentious and vulgar, being resorted to frequently in too great haste; prompted more by emotion and fear, than by common sense, and certainly lacking in charity, as the following example demonstrates: 'At Bath you have known the Simkinses, and even been intimate with them, but in Town you take it into your head they are "inferior", you meet and cut them. Well, a fortnight later, you find that Lady So-and-so is particularly partial to the Simkinses.'[10]

The practice of 'cutting' being countenanced by society, it seems that some definite rules or what, or what not, to do were not thought amiss. A cut was to be made 'with as little offensiveness as possible'. Thus, the individual was allowed to see that his approach had been noticed – 'then turn your head away', is the advice tendered. It should never reach the necessity of saying: 'I do not know you'; or even: 'I have not the honour of your acquaintance'. By no means everyone, however, could claim the distinction of being able to use the cut. A woman could cut another woman or a man, though unmarried women were not supposed to cut married ones on any account. Men could not cut women. Near relations obviously abstained from the practice among themselves, and those in any form of service, of whatever class, even to royalty itself, could not cut their masters. Clergymen had no right to cut anyone at all – 'because it is at best an unchristian action'; while doctors, however great was their dislike of one another, 'should never introduce the "cut" over the bed of a patient'.[10]

10 *The Habits of Good Society*. London, *c.* 1860. pp. 276–80.

(b) SALUTATIONS

'A gentleman, who is acquainted with life, enters a room with gracefulness and a modest assurance, addresses even persons he does not know in an easy and natural manner, and without the least embarrassment. This is the characteristic of good breeding, a very necessary knowledge in our intercourse with men; for, one of inferior parts, with the behaviour of a gentleman, is frequently better received than a man of sense with the address and manners of a clown.'[11]

'Gracefulness and a modest assurance': these characteristics have, since Graeco-Roman times, been part of the polish associated with city-bred people. To this conception, indeed, we owe words like polite (πολρ), urbane (*urbs*), and civility (*civis*), in contrast to the uncouth countryman (*rusticus*). The acquisition of the qualities which go to the making of a 'gentleman' were taken for granted among those who moved in well-bred society in the nineteenth century. Above all things vulgarity of outward display, including over-punctiliousness of manner, was 'bad style'; and to be in 'bad style' was to be damned.

The Bow

Early in the century, the bow and curtsy disappeared except on formal occasions, and the hand-shake now became the accepted form of greeting. First, though, we should see how these ancient forms of salutation, so long practised in the polite world, were performed in this new era of industrial revolution.

Bows and curtsies were used mostly in the ballroom, where they were introduced into certain figures of dances, and where the man made a slight bow when inviting his partner to dance. From the fifteenth century and earlier every dance had begun and ended with a reverence. In consequence, authors of dance treatises described them as carefully as the dances themselves. 'We no longer hold it indispensable that the lesson should commence with a courtesy or formal bow', wrote a

[11] Earl of Car: *The New Chesterfield*. London, 1830.

dancing master in 1847. 'A pupil who is able to execute with
tolerable perfection these modern dances, which I do not fear
to call natural, will of himself know how to walk, bow, and
present himself with grace. The master has little or nothing to
do with these details.'[12]

Nevertheless, during the earlier decades of the century there
were still directions on how to make a bow or curtsy, in the
various manuals of ballroom dancing (as it had come to be
called) and in books of etiquette (Appendix I(g) i and ii).

The Curtsy and Introductions

The Young Lady's Book, published in 1829, ran to six editions
in a few years. The reprint of 1859, with fashions in dress
brought up to date, shows that the instructions for deportment remained the same. 'The perfect curtsy', it says, 'is rarely
performed in society, as the general salutation is between a
curtsy and a bow.' (Fig. 11.) In 1860 it was said that 'except
in the third figure of the Lancers, and in the presence of
royalty, curtsys are seldom performed. In the latter case, it
is scarcely possible, consistent with etiquette, to bend too
low'.

It was always the lady's place to give the first intimation
of recognition. After seeing that the gentleman was looking
towards her, she bowed very slightly with the head and
shoulders. To raise her glasses in order to ascertain whether or
not he was the person she supposed him to be, was ill-mannered,
yet she could not risk bowing to a stranger. It could be
embarrassing for the short-sighted lady.

The man waited until the lady bowed to him, then lifted his
hat from his head with the hand farthest from her, to avoid
masking his face with his arm, while bending the body slightly
forward (Fig. 12). Should he be smoking, he quickly removed
his cigar from his mouth. The Englishman merely lifted his
hat off his head, immediately replacing it. The Frenchman
brought the hat down in front – 'to show the world the inside
thereof'.

Should the gentleman and lady be no more than mere
acquaintances, he should not offer to shake her hand unless

---

[12] Cellarius: *The Drawing Room Dances.* London, 1847.

FIG. 11   The lady's curtsy in the nineteenth century.
The Young Lady's Book. 1829. (*British Museum*)

she first offered hers. If they were well acquainted, the man at once offered his hand to her, as he would do to another man. On leaving, he again raised his hat, bowing as before.

Should two ladies, walking together, meet a gentleman known to only one of the ladies, both would pause, whereupon she who knew the gentleman would introduce him to her friend. 'Such an introduction is merely formal and goes no farther.' A gentleman was reminded, too, that following a ball, 'an introduction given for the mere purpose of enabling a lady and gentleman to go through a dance together, does not constitute an acquaintanceship. The lady is at liberty to pass the gentleman in the park the next day without recognition. No

gentleman should venture to bow to a lady upon the strength
of a ball-room introduction, unless she does him the honour
to recognize him first. If he commits this solecism, he must not
be surprised to find that she does not return his salutation'.[13]

Shaking hands

Although during the first two or three decades of the nineteenth century the formalities of bowing and curtsying had
not quite disappeared from everyday convention, the estab-

[13] Anon: *The Ballroom Companion*. London, 1860.

FIG. 12   Men raising their hats, using the hand away from
the person saluted. *Habits of Good Society*. c. 1860.
(*British Museum*)

lished mode of greeting was to shake hands. Hence the correct way of doing this began to occupy the attention of all who proffered advice on good manners – extending even to modern times.

Thomas Tegg, for example, gave the matter detailed consideration when he wrote his *A Present for an Apprentice* in 1838. 'Shaking hands is an expressive and affectionate mode of salutation and parting, but it should be done in a proper manner. There is an affectionate and a refined manner, and there is a cold and awkward manner of shaking hands, as well as of doing other things. Many people obtain their first and most abiding impressions of a stranger from his manner of performing this salutation. You must generally take the hand of a stranger with more reserve than that of an acquaintance, unless he is introduced by some esteemed friend; for whatever familiar warmth of interest you then express, is for your friend's sake. But never receive the hand even of a stranger with coldness or suspicion. Do it with a sincere though reserved cordiality. But the hand of a well-known friend can hardly be seized with too much affection, provided you sincerely feel it. . . . When you approach a person to shake hands with him . . . throw your kindling and gladdened eye right into his, and give him your hand at once without any preliminary flourish.'[14]

'The most cordial way of shaking hands is to give both at once.' Even the simple act of shaking hands can reveal oddities of character. For example, 'the pouncing style of him who affects but does not feel cordiality, who brings the angle between thumb and finger down upon you like gaping shears'. And 'the style of man who gives your hand one toss, as if he were ringing the dinner bell', or 'the solemn style, where the elbow is tucked into the side, like the wing of a trussed fowl, and the long fingers are extended with the thumb in close attendance'. There is 'Milady, who shakes her own hand from the wrist with a neat fine little movement, and does not care whether yours shakes in it or not', and a favourite mode with young ladies, if they are not well acquainted with a person, was to give the hand 'clammily in the other, which slightly presses the fingers'.[15]

[14] Tegg: *A Present for an Apprentice*.
[15] Anon: *The Habits of Good Society*. pp. 185 and 186.

The etiquette of shaking hands was simple. No man would take a lady's hand unless she first offered hers. It was polite for a lady to rise in order to give her hand, while the gentleman would never offer his when seated. Two ladies generally shook hands 'gently and softly', and 'a young lady gives her hand, but does not shake a gentleman's unless she is his friend'. 'On introduction in a room, a married lady generally offers her hand, a young lady not; in a ballroom, where the introduction is to dancing, not to friendship, you never shake hands; and as a general rule, an introduction is not followed by shaking hands, only by a bow. It may perhaps be laid down, that the more public the place on introduction, the less hand-shaking takes place; but if the introduction be particular, if it is accompanied by a personal recommendation, such as "I want you to know my friend, Jones," or, if Jones comes with a letter of presentation, then you give Jones your hand, and warmly too. Lastly, it is the privilege of a superior to offer or withold his hand, so that an inferior should never put his forward first.'[16]

In earlier days, when the salutation was a bow rather than a hand-shake, it had been the practice for juniors, or inferiors, to pay the first honour to those above them.

In polite society the French were still regarded by many as the masters of fashion and etiquette, and from them the English borrowed various conventions of social formality. There remained differences, of course, between the customs and manners of the two countries. In some cases, the French were slower to reject the formalities of earlier times than were the English. The slight inclination of the head, used by ladies in place of the curtsy, and what was termed 'the American shake-hand', were disliked by the French. As late as the mid-nineteenth century, shaking hands between the sexes – particularly between a man and a young girl – was permitted in France only after the two had been acquainted for some time. 'Englishmen are undeniably the most conservative men in the world, and in nothing do they shew it more universally than in maintaining their usual habits in any country, climate, or season. . . . Excellent, for instance, is the custom of shaking hands, but it has on the Continent generally

16 ibid., p. 287.

a much more friendly and particular signification. . . . In fact, a French *jeune fille* never takes a gentleman's hand unless he is quite an *ami de la maison*, so that for an Englishman at a first visit to shake hands all round, amounts to a familiarity.'[17]

This shows that with the French, the traditional significance of the handclasp had persisted. In this single custom we see again the long shadow of the past upon the present and the way in which the history of gesture, still new as a branch of knowledge, can deepen understanding of national psychology and the emotional development of mankind.

(c) HOSTS AND GUESTS

Visiting cards

A form of visiting card was used by the ancient Egyptians for presentation at the temples where they worshipped. These were a kind of glazed tile upon which was depicted the figure of a man together with his titles. Thus, as artificial a custom as the use of calling cards had its origin in religious ceremonial.

In Europe, visiting cards became an established fashion at the French court of Louis XIV, although they were probably in use much earlier. Towards the end of the eighteenth century, the custom was adopted by fashionable society throughout Europe, including England. 'There are many great men who go unrewarded for the services they render to humanity. . . . One of these is he, if it was not a lady, who introduced the use of visiting cards', is the grandoise claim made in a work published about the middle of the century. It seems that in times past visitors who found their friends 'not at home', wrote their names in a book or on a slate. 'To the French is due the practice of making the delivery of a card serve the purpose of the appearance of the individual, and with those who have a large acquaintance, this custom is becoming very common in large towns.' Thus it was that the tedium of paying endless visits was replaced, at least for the husband, by the etiquette of the visiting card.

During the nineteenth century, and for about the first quarter of the twentieth, the etiquette of 'calling' was a firmly

17 ibid., p. 137.

observed rule of society. The visiting card was essential. In-
scribed in copper-plate were the name and titles of the visitor.
The address might be placed in the bottom corner. Titles, except
honorary or business titles, were used, otherwise the majority
put 'Mr' or 'Mrs' in front of their names. Slim card cases, sometimes made of silver, and which could slip easily into a pocket,
were a convenience.

The manner of calling

Since many more persons of polite society in this century
were engaged in business than in earlier periods, the husband
was considered too busy to spare the time for visiting. So the
ceremony of calling devolved as a rule on the wife who took
her husband's cards with her. A caller left one card for the
lady of the house and for her grown-up daughter (or daughters).
To indicate that the daughters were included, one edge of the
card was turned up. A second card was left for the master of
the house, and should there be a grown-up son, or near male
relative in the house, a third card was left. Newcomers to a
town or village waited until they had received a call from
inhabitants of longer standing; then, after a suitable interval.
they returned the call, following which the process of re-
ciprocal entertaining could begin.

A Gentleman caller

If a gentleman wished to call upon a family, his call would
be made upon the lady of the house, not upon the master,
unless it was merely a business call. If he learned from the
servant who opened the door, that the mistress was not at
home, but that a daughter was in, the gentleman would leave
his card, 'because young ladies do not receive calls from
gentlemen, unless they are very intimate with them or have
passed the rubicon of thirty summers'. If, however, the lady
was at home, the gentleman would be ushered upstairs to the
drawing-room, and here he must know the etiquette of what
to take up with him – such as coat or cane – and what to leave
downstairs.

Greatcoats, it seems, were not worn much in nineteenth-
century England. It was not a convenient garment for visiting,

because in England it was not the custom to remove it and leave it downstairs; in fact, when worn, it had to be buttoned up. Weather permitting, it was easier to do without it[18] If the gentleman caller carried an umbrella, this was left downstairs in the hall. His hat and cane were taken up to the drawing-room, for a call of this nature was to be a short visit, and to leave these downstairs implied that he intended to stay longer, which would be contrary to good manners. During the visit, the hat was to be held in the hand 'gracefully'. It was not to be placed upon a chair or table, but, if it was necessary for him to have both hands free, he had to put it on the floor, close to his chair.

The time for calling

It was considerate to avoid calling in the morning, when most people were busy. The practice of evening visits was adopted from the French, but during the social whirl of the 'Season', this could be unrewarding, most people being out at that time. Afternoon visits were favoured more, or, best of all, the use of a fixed visiting day.

Introductions

The age-old custom of leading a guest by the hand out of courtesy, was out of fashion; 'In introducing two persons, it is not necessary to lead one of them up by the hand; it is sufficient simply to precede them.' Having brought the two persons face to face, the one making the introduction said, with a slight bow to the superior or elder of the two, 'Will you allow me to introduce Mr——?' The person so addressed then bowed slightly to whoever was being introduced to him, who also bowed in reply; meanwhile the introducer repeated both names again before leaving them to talk. In large towns, on the occasion of a fixed visiting day, the fact that a number of people would be assembled in their host's house, was considered to be sufficient introduction. In this case, it was thought unnecessary to introduce people to one another. In the greater

---

[18] According to Thomas Tegg, the gentleman did leave his cloak, or greatcoat, in the hall. But Tegg was writing for a middle-class readership. Those who could not afford their own carriage would find greatcoats a necessity.

intimacy of country-house gatherings, introductions were usual. Moreover the English, being somewhat reserved, did not take kindly to this latest continental fashion of doing without an introduction.

LADIES

The lady's visiting-dress was synonymous with her carriage-dress, for no lady would entertain the notion of walking on such an occasion. Even when dressed for walking, it was considered 'ungenteel' to wear anything but thin shoes, or very light boots, which meant that the old-fashioned clog, or galosh, had still to be worn as outdoor protection. The inhabitants of *Cranford* were said to clatter home 'in their pattens under the guidance of a lantern-bearer'. In *Cranford* 'there were rules and regulations for visiting and calling'. It was said that never should 'more than three days elapse between receiving a call and returning it', and that on no account should the visit be 'longer than a quarter of an hour'. This made it necessary to keep thinking about the time, so they were to keep themselves 'to short sentences of small talk', and remain punctual as to time.[19]

Even in those days of greater leisure, the practice of visiting could be a strain upon the ladies of the house. 'Some underbred ladies in country towns', it seems, had not the *savoir-faire* to conceal their impatience from their visitors, showing 'symptoms of hurry and preoccupation'; sometimes glancing out of the window, or tidying their work-boxes, or even allowing a servant to announce that their carriage was ready to take them out.

French and English hostesses

The French habit of a fixed calling day disposed of much of this vexation; the French hostess was said to possess an easier manner towards her guests, making them feel that they did her an honour. Some English ladies were casual in their behaviour. When the guest rose to depart, they contented themselves with ringing for a servant, then sat down to resume a conversation before the guest had time barely to cross the room.

[19] Mrs Gaskell: *Cranford, and other Tales.* London, 1851–3.

Parasols

A lady did not carry her umbrella into the drawing-room, but the very small, elegant parasols were decorative enough to be kept in the hand. Sometimes an elegantly worked handkerchief could be held in the hand, but this was more suitable for dinner parties.

Chairs

Guests no longer sought the least honoured chair, though no one would want to occupy a favoured position at the expense of others. 'In good society, a visitor, unless he is a complete stranger, does not wait to be invited to sit down, but takes a seat at once, easily.'

Invitations to stay at a house

An invitation to stay at a country house was sent always by the hostess, not the host. The wording of the invitation was made, and acted upon, with care. Generally a visit was expected to last three days; the guest arriving for dinner in the evening of the first day, and leaving either after lunch, or before dinner, of the third. This could be indicated by the words 'Come and stay with us a few days'. 'Come and stay with us a few weeks' was not to be taken too literally; a week was a fair period. A general invitation was never to be acted upon; it was often given with no intention of following it up. At a country house, the hostess either sent her own carriage, or hired a 'fly' to meet the guest at the station. On leaving, the visitor often made his own arrangements. It was 'bad taste to arrive with a waggonful of luggage', indicating a lengthy stay.

Servants and children on visits

From medieval times, it had been the custom for guests to bring their own servants to wait upon them. As late as the nineteenth century, it was not unusual for a valet or lady's maid to accompany the master or mistress, but by the middle of the century the fashion was dying out, except with royalty and the aristocracy. 'If a gentleman cannot dispense with his valet, or a lady with her maid, they should write to ask leave to bring a servant; but the means of your inviter, and the size of the house should be taken into consideration, and it is better taste to dispense with a servant altogether.'[20]

As for arriving with children and horses, these were even more awkward for the hosts, and to arrive without special mention of them in advance, would be in still worse taste.

Tips

Although hospitality in those days was lavish, the guests had their problems concerning the expense involved in such visits. 'The worst part of a country visit is the necessity of giving gratuities to the servants, for a poor man may often find his visit cost him far more than if he had stayed at home. In a great house, a man-servant expects gold, but a poor man should not be ashamed of offering him silver. It must depend on the length of the visit.'[21] It was the habit for the men to tip the male servants, and for the ladies to give to the females.

[20] Anon: *The Habits of Good Society.* p. 298.
[21] ibid., p. 299.

CHAPTER VII

The Twentieth Century

(a) PRE–1914–18 WAR: (b) POST–WAR

Pre-war

In early works on manners and deportment prominence was given to the gentleman, especially in his position as host. In the nineteenth century a slight change is noticeable in that the lady becomes the particular target towards which maxims of good behaviour were directed. From the opening years of the twentieth century contemporary books of etiquette give a much greater share of attention to the lady – as the 'hostess'.

Basic rules of good manners, from which spring fashions of social etiquette, were founded in times far removed from the present day; yet links with the past are still seen. They are more apparent in those circles which, because of their position in society, are obliged to conform more closely to accepted norms of social conduct: the royal and aristocratic households, and to a lesser degree the homes also of the upper classes have been those in which the continuity of traditional behaviour can be seen more clearly.

The teaching of manners begins in childhood, and in the households of the aristocracy and the upper classes this usually started with the child's nurse: 'As was customary in those days, a British "nannie" was an indispensable part of all royal nurseries,' wrote Princess Marie Louise. In these circles the inculcation of good manners was regarded as an important part of education.

The traditional upbringing of children and young persons in the upper classes, at least up to the outbreak of the 1914-18 war, was based firmly on discipline, starting in the nursery and continuing under tutors and governesses. At all times in the presence of grown-ups, whether members of the family or visitors, children were taught to 'behave properly'. Their pocket-money – to be spent as they wished – was frugal. The custom, which went back to Medieval times, whereby children were educated at home or in some private household, was continued for far longer in the case of girls' education. Princess Marie Louise, speaking of her own upbringing, says that young girls were educated at home, and that governesses superintended and taught them, and that they also chaperoned them whenever the girls attended outside classes or lectures. In the days of which she spoke – from about the early to mid-eighteen-eighties – the idea 'that girls should go to boarding-schools, let alone colleges, was unheard of, and I think our fond Mamas would have had fits – to put it mildly – if they had entrusted their precious offspring to the care of strangers'. But this by no means meant that girls of the upper classes were uneducated. In addition to their being taught the usual subjects of the school curriculum, Princess Marie Louise says that they had a resident German governess, also twice-weekly lessons in French literature and European history. There were dancing classes and physical drill, both in order to know how to dance and to achieve good health and good deportment. It seems that her father considered deportment to be an important part of girls' education. 'We had to learn how to stand, how to rise, how to sit down (gracefully), how to walk, and above all how to bow and curtsey and greet people and crowds with a little wave of the hand, a smile, and what I can only describe as a slight inclination of the head.'

There was at first great opposition to any change in women's education or occupation. Miss Beale, who became Principal of Ladies College, Cheltenham in 1858, and Miss Buss of the North London Collegiate School for Ladies (1850), had to fight the conventional ideas about schooling for young ladies of the upper classes; the opponents of the new ideas feared that learning which followed the same lines as that already taught to boys might be injurious to female brains.

While the 'should be seen and not heard' attitude towards children was now widely condemned, the swing to the opposite extreme may not prove as kind as the intention appears to be. The normal training of the young for adult life, particularly in artistocratic and upper class circles, in previous generations leaned towards self-disciplined conduct. The over-scrupulous conventions of society life in the nineteenth and early twentieth century would have been felt more burdensome had childhood training been based on *laisser aller*.

At home in upper middle class households children, especially girls, were expected to lend a hand in some household chores such as making their beds, washing-up, 'doing' their own room. The fact of having servants did not absolve children from these small duties.

We who live in the late twentieth century are conscious, especially today, that society consists of many shades of class distinctions, all of which have their specific form of social behaviour – a kind of secret code recognized instinctively by members of any particular group. To dub certain behaviour as belonging to one section of the population would be too dogmatic, but as the upbringing of children and youth of any section of the populace affects us all, it may be of interest to note the opinion of a writer of working-class origin concerning the treatment of children as he knew it in the particular community with which he was familiar. He writes (in 1957): 'They do mishandle their children by "educated" standards; I mean by the standards usually advocated in modern books on childcare. It is a working-class tradition of long standing to indulge not only children but young people all the way up to marriage: there is all the rest of life to come and you cannot do much about that; you must let them 'ave a good time while they can; after all, "yer' only young once".[1] These contrasting class attitudes, influenced perhaps by the knowledge that adult life for the one would be hard and for the other less hard, could be expected to change as times and conditions change, but traditions of behaviour are slow to alter.

The concept of social class has been accepted without question from distant-times. At one time a person's 'position' in life was regarded rather in the light of a God-given Order of Mankind; as a fact of existence; all-pervading throughout society and so reflected in literature, including children's books. 'Knowing one's place' was a widely used expression.

From earliest times different categories of work have borne

[1] Richard Hoggart: *The Uses of Literacy*. Chatto and Windus, 1957.

M

the distinctions of 'class'. It has been said that the Greeks' love
of physical beauty gave them a dislike for manual labour as
being work which made a person acquire a stoop, or caused
their limbs and hands to become mis-shapen or begrimed.

Cicero had firm ideas concerning the trades which were suitable or unsuitable for the ruling classes. Any trade which
tended to make persons disliked, such as usurers and tax
gatherers were 'unworthy'; so, too, were 'those arts (which)
are mean and ungenteel, in which a man is paid for his work,
not his skill.'[2]

The demarcation lines between employment thought to be
socially acceptable for the upper classes and that which was
regarded as beneath the line were at one time even extended
to the diversions which were considered suited to a person's
social position. In a work dated 1838 addressed to an apprentice,[3] it is stated that 'Music is another of those accomplishments which are generally quite superfluous in such a station
as yours; nay, not only useless, but absolutely detrimental:
to have one's head filled with crochets being a proverbial phrase
to denote a man beside himself'. The professions became the
occupation considered suitable in general for the upper classes,
whereas a career in 'trade' was thought to be in the social
sense more doubtful.

Post-war

The holocaust of the 1914–18 war caused a temporary cessa-
tion of the social events which are the *raison d'etre* of books
of etiquette. A year or two after the end of the war the rules
found in pre-war editions were again propounded, as though
there was a desire to return to what had been normal
previously. But at the end of the Twenties there enters a new
feeling. It is pointed out that constant revision has to be made
in order to keep the newly published work up to date: 'In
particular', as the manual adds, 'attention has been paid to the
changes in social customs that have taken place in Post-War
Society, and care has been taken to indicate to what extent the
strict rules of etiquette are still enforced and in what circumstances they may be regarded as optional'.

[2] Cicero: *Offices, Essays and Letters.* J. M. Dent and Sons, London.
[3] *'A Present for an Apprentice* by the Late T. Tegg Esq'. London, 1838.

(a) SOCIAL ETIQUETTE AND CHANGING CUSTOMS

The Lady: Pre-war

Apart from her casting an eye over the running of her house (by servants) unless she employed a housekeeper, and the care of her children (in the hands of nurses or governesses), the main ocupation for a lady at this period was concerned with numerous social engagements. There were certain duties which could be undertaken such as visiting the sick and the poor to distribute gifts – a custom of long standing in the wealthy or aristocratic families, and which was imitated in upper class households. Hints of Moral Deportment given to a young lady of the nineteenth century would follow much the same lines in the early twentieth century: 'Whether you are the mistress of a regular allowance, or the proprietor of casual sums, never fail to appropriate some portion of your pocket-money to a charity purse. . . . Do not forget that Charity has a much wider signification than alms-giving. Affability of manners; gentleness of demeanour; attention to the courtesies of life; compassion towards all who suffer, whether high or low'. 'We were taught to work for the sick and distressed,' wrote Princess Marie Louise, 'and I can still remember, at the age of six, trying to roll a bandage which was destined to be sent out to the sick and wounded in the Russo-Turkish War of 1878.'

This gentility of existence, in which women's occupation largely consisted of needlework, paying social calls (or charitable ones), acquiring the correct small-talk for brief social visits, was soon to change beyond recognition.

The first significant stirring towards the emancipation of women began in the nineteenth century; from the opening of the present century the movement gathered pace. From about the mid-nineteenth century various developments brought about a new outlook regarding women's place in society. Ideas concerning schooling for girls underwent a fundamental change during the second half of the century. Education for girls of the upper classes, which for years had been in the hands of governesses employed in private residences, was now considered to be more suitably achieved at school, even, as time passed, at boarding-school.

In the outside world, too, there grew an increasing awareness of the work which women were well able to do, pointing to the opportunity of a life beyond the restricted home-environment: notably and foremost was the service of nursing. The Crimean and South African wars brought into being organized nursing staffs, partly professional and partly voluntary. The (Voluntary Aid Detachment) V.A.Ds. was started in 1909, and in September 1914, following the outbreak of the 1914-18 War, the Women's Hospital Corps was responsible for opening a hospital for Allied troops in Paris. Then indeed were young nurses, many of whom had come from sheltered backgrounds of upper- and middle-class homes, thrown into contact with the frightfulness of war. As the war progressed, so the numbers of women drafted into the Services grew in their hundreds: there was the Women's Auxiliary Corps, the Women's Royal Naval Service, the Women's Royal Air Force. Civilian services such as the Women's Police Service also came into being. Then too came Women's Suffrage and its counter movements: The National Women's Social and Political Union (associated especially with Mrs and Christobel Pankhurst) and the Men's League for Opposing Women's Suffrage, and so on, during the first decade of the twentieth century.

All these new devolpments were bound to affect the long-established tenor of life for women, thus inevitably affecting their outlook, which in turn would be reflected in their general deportment, and not least in the attitude of their menfolk to those changing circumstances.

These upheavals, however, did not directly affect the everyday existence of the majority of women, for whom the daily routine of housewifery and social engagements continued much the same as in the previous half century. High on the list came the firmly established duty of Paying Calls. The tedium of paying courtesy visits had been noted by a gentleman of the seventeenth century; by the twentieth century, this social duty had become almost entirely the province of the feminine world, except of course in the case of bachelors.

The Lady: Post-war

The change in fashion and outlook concerning women brought about by the First World War was more startling than any of which we have a record. In addition to the effect of the war, another factor was a new attitude towards physical culture and sport for women. From the eighties and nineties of the previous century, tennis, golf, bicycling and other sports had had an increasing influence upon women's clothes, resulting in more freedom of movement for the wearer. Throughout the Twenties and Thirties classes for physical recreation and fitness increased steadily in popularity. ' "Keep Fit" classes are multiplying, and girls and women are showing themselves to be as enthusiastic as their brothers and husbands for open-air games and pastimes, where the opportunity is given them to take part. . . . Women today recognize that exercise as well as food, sleep, fresh air, and cleanliness, is one of the necessities of a healthy life. . . . This general desire for physical activity should be guided to the best advantage.'[4] The 'Keep Fit' cult became 'news' and big demonstrations were held, Prunella Stack being prominent as a leader of the movement.

Such activities had their effect on the physique of growing girls whose schooling now included physical training (P.T.) and various outdoor games. No longer were girls and women regarded as somewhat frail beings, moving throughout their daily occupations with appropriate gentility. One result of this bodily exercise was that girls tended to grow in stature, becoming taller, stronger, and more active; it was noticeable, too, that in women's clothes and footwear larger sizes came into demand. The evidence of this change in physique is seen clearly in women's dresses of the nineteenth century which are usually so much smaller. The heroine in a contemporary magazine story of the Twenties was visualized now more as a companion whose lithe figure 'swung down the lane, with a spaniel at her heels'. The erstwhile soft, lady-like handshake could, in some cases, now become a hearty gymnastic-style grip.

A perusal of *Punch* of the early post-war years bears ample witness to the gay enthusiasm of the contemporary young woman for all kinds of sport, physical culture and dancing

[4] *Recreation and Physical Fitness for Girls and Women.* Board of Education PT Series No. 16, HMSO, 1937.

(whether expressive Eurythmics or vigorous ballroom dancing). Amongst a series of illustrations, in the Summer Number
of 1921, entitled *Eighty Years of Change* (1841 to 1921), the
vast change that had taken place during these years is depicted.
Here the prim, crinolined figure of 1841, playing croquet, had
given place to a short-skirted girl about to volley a tennis
ball; ladies bathing from a machine at the surf's edge, with a
gentleman looking the other way, were replaced in 1921 by a
girl in a brief bathing suit lighting a young man's cigarette;
and a speed-hog on a motor-cyce with his girl riding pillion
(then in side-saddle style!) were the descendants of a sedate
couple walking arm-in-arm, with a chaperon following at a
discreet distance. More often than not, the bright young women
of the day were satirized in *Punch* as having little real understanding of the sports they had so enthusiastically embraced:
Illustration of two ladies:

> '*I hear you've taken up golf. What do you go round in?*'
> *Young woman golfer:* '*Well, usually in a jumper.*'
> *(Punch, April 1921)*

Before the First World War women's stockings were not
attractive: often black woollen or cotton, white cotton, or
grey (sometimes white) silk for smarter occasions; but, as the
stockings were barely seen, this was of little consequence. As
late as the early Twenties recipe books gave amongst their
general hints a method whereby black stockings could be
prevented from turning green in the wash. The bottom edge
of ladies' skirts were edged with a band of special material to
prevent the hems from wearing out, and these long skirts required constant brushing after being worn out of doors.

In photographs of the year 1917 hospital nurses are shown in
long ankle-length white dresses, and uniforms, such as that
of the Women's Police Service, also had their skirts *raised*
to the ankle – a length thought to be quite daring.

> *No more her dainty feet, I note*
> '*Like little mice*' *(as Suckling wrote)*
> *Peep from the modest petticoat.*
> *No need, when I her ankle see,*
> *Her Fancy for to convey to me*
> *How fair the leg above must be.* (O.S.)
> *(Punch, June 1921, Owen Seaman)*

By 1919 skirts had become much shorter. Communication with countries abroad were not as easy in those days, particularly in wartime, and items such as the newest fashions in dress took time to find their way to the outposts of the Empire. To those returning to their home-land at the end of the war, the sudden confrontation with the newly short-skirted women was quite arresting. Nor were skirts the main alteration in women's dress: in the early to mid Twenties, the tight-belted waist-band to dresses and skirts, with the strongly boned corset beneath, had disappeared into history, and the fashion for knee-length waistless dresses, not unlike pillow slips, was adopted. It was fashionable during the mid Twenties for women's figures to appear to be flat both in front and behind, which suited these shapeless clothes. With this there was adopted by some fashion-conscious women a pose in which the hips were pushed forwards, eliminating any natural curve behind. This attitude could accompany the long cigarette holder, and a conscious display of leg from the knee down, in fashionably shaded silk, or very fine cotton, stockings.

> (The fashion-Press states that all shades of
> amber are now popular for ladies' hose).
> When she displays her yellow hose
> He simply tells her, with a laugh,
> That now he sees why there arose
> The worship of the Golden Calf.
> (Punch, June 1921)

These poses may have been influenced by the stage, where these attitudes were presented, for it is a little difficult now to judge whether poses attributed to the Bright Young Things of the Twenties were a part of every-day life of whether the rather stage-struck young fashionables were copying exaggerations seen on stage. The Twenties were a great period for the theatre – including the cinema, which was then the most widely patronized form of entertainment for old and young alike, since the standard of films shown at this time had greatly improved from earlier examples. Actors and actresses, who also appeared on the London stage, were brought through films regularly before the public. The names of many film actors and actresses thus became household words throughout the country, and fashions favoured by these popular 'stars' were copied by their fans. Instead of the lead in fashion-styles being set by the Court and high society, as in the past, this influence passed to the idols of the film world.

More and more women began to take an active part in varied walks of life: teaching, nursing, the Law, even politics. In spite of this the idea, which is accepted without question today, that on leaving school a girl should train for some particular work did not find general approval. In many families girls stayed at home (until they married) where they gave a helping hand (thereby learning something of housekeeping) and took part in the usual social round. But this way of life was no longer easy to maintain. Rising prices, and in many cases the loss of the breadwinner through wartime casualties, made it necessary for girls from some families to earn their keep. For many young women the prospect of marriage in the years following the 1914–18 war was not favourable because of the consequent preponderance of women in the country.

As women began to compete with men in the every-day routine of 'a job', so by degrees the habits of long-established courtesies, such as a man giving up his seat in the crowded 'rush-hour' train to a lady, changed. It was inevitable that men and women now had to be equals in the fatigue of daily work and travel.

The Gentleman

Outward forms of behaviour did not alter throughout the later nineteenth and early twentieth century as markedly with men as with women for whom the greater restraint in social conduct was largely intended as a safeguard to the 'frail sex'. Men's dress had not undergone the abrupt changes of fashion which in many instances had restricted movement as, for example, the crinoline, the bustle, very long sweeping skirts, shorter skirts, hobble skirts and the like. On the contrary, men's bearing and habits had for some years mostly followed accepted standards of behaviour influenced to a large extent by public school codes.

There were inevitable changes, of course, in small matters of etiquette as that of the correct procedure when paying a social call. Whereas in former times 'a gentleman took his hat and stick in his hand with him into the drawing-room, and held them until he had seen the mistress of the house and shaken hands with her' he now followed 'the newer fashion among younger men' who left their hats and sticks in the hall. Many middle-aged and elderly men still kept to the old tradition, but 'hats are in the way if tea is going on, besides which men were apt to forget where they had placed their hats, and frequently had to return to the drawing-room in search of them'.

'Intellectual workers', artists and men of letters were forgiven occasional 'minor solecisms in dress and manners' on account of their fame and talents, but ordinary individuals had to conform and follow the prescribed rules of fashion.

So it will be seen that the everyday codes of polite conduct have changed but imperceptibly. It was still considered a part of good upbringing for a man to know 'how to enter a room, how to bow and how to dress'; and also, when entering a theatre, concert-room or crowded place, that the gentleman should precede the lady, to clear the way for her and to show her to her seat. When walking with a lady in the street the age-old custom of giving the lady the wall (putting her between the wall and himself) was still observed. A gentleman removed his hat on entering a private residence out of respect for his host or hostess, but he would do so in a public place such as a shop or hotel entrance only if he expected to meet a lady who was a friend or acquaintance.

Although social barriers marking distinctive 'sets' were still in evidence after the 1914–18 War, men were noticeably less mindful of the virtue of their observance than applied in the case of women. Among a man's friends 'reciprocity of taste' was the basis of friendship, and this in some degree implied a similarity of social status.

(b) SALUTATIONS

Shaking hands

Advice given in manuals of conventional conduct in the early Twenties clearly states that 'the etiquette with regard to shaking hands is not an open question, it is distinct enough and simple enough for all exigencies, but yet there is individual temperament to be taken into account which, in many, drives etiquette out of the field, if by etiquette is understood not merely stiff propriety of action, but politeness in the truest sense of the word, and in doing that which is exactly the right thing to do. Etiquette rules when to shake hands and when not to do so, when to bow and when not to bow; but in spite of this knowledge, which is within everyone's reach, there are many mistakes on this head'.

A lady, in her capacity as a hostess, would shake hands with everyone who was presented to her in her own home. People who were being introduced to one another, generally expressed their recognition of this with a slight bow; this applied to both men and women, particularly in the case of persons unknown to one another. Should whoever was being introduced happen to be a friend or relative of the introducer, a bow would appear to be too distant and the parties would then shake hands. It was the privilege of an elderly lady, or perhaps one of higher rank, to offer her hand, a gesture taken as a compliment and mark of friendliness. There were some who betrayed their lack of good breeding even in this simple act, as the lady to gave 'but two fingers to people whom she [did] not care about; she [was] always a person who fancied herself and who felt very fine'.

Another fashion of former times among ladies had been that of 'raising the arm when shaking hands. . . . It found favour with very few and was generally considered bad style. The correct way is to offer the hand, on a line parallel with the chest, a trifle higher perhaps than the old-fashioned style, and the fingers of the hand are held and gently shaken, but the palm is not grasped or even touched'.

By the late Twenties the advice concerning shaking hands was less assured than formerly: 'When to shake hands and when not to do so is somewhat of an open question . . . but there are certain occasions on which it is usual to shake hands and others when it is not'. In general, it was said, 'when in doubt it is better not to do so'.

Introductions

The correct manner of introducing people to one another depended upon social position, rank, age and the sex of the parties concerned. Where there was a difference of status between two persons, whoever was of lower rank was introduced to the other by having his, or her, name given first; the same applied to difference in age, the younger being introduced to the elder. Unmarried ladies were regarded as having lower status than married ladies, unless the former happened to be of higher social rank, and the gentleman, no matter whether he was of high rank or not, was always introduced to the lady.

It was customary to ask a lady's consent before introducing someone to her, but with men this was not necessary unless the occasion was a ball or dance when the introduction was for the purpose of dancing: in this case the inquiry was made because, if the man was unable to follow the introduction with an invitation to the lady to dance, the situation might be somewhat embarrassing for both parties. On the other hand, because introductions at a ball were made for the purpose of dancing, and not for social acquaintance, it was unnecessary to ask the lady's permission before introducing a gentleman; the lady could, with as much courtesy as possible, plead some excuse in refusing the invitation should she so wish.

The question of making introductions required tact, particularly in the early Twenties when consciousness of social class was observed more rigidly than in later years. It was not always wise to act on the assumption that ladies who moved in different social circles would wish to be introduced to one another.

At Morning or Afternoon social visits, also at Evening parties, formal introductions were no longer made unless there was a particular reason for doing so; the guests took for granted that, as the company present were friends of their host and hostess, this formality was unnecessary. Only a few old-fashioned country hosts, persevered in the former custom, which put the last visitor in an unenviable position.

The Bow and the Curtsy

When meeting friends and acquaintances out of doors the usual form of recognition was for the lady to bow and the

man to take off his hat. The curtsy, performed in times past
with elaborate care, was no longer used as a form of greeting.
In some figures of certain dances the couples made an
occasional bow and curtsy, and they were always made to
royalty by those who were being presented.

The man's bow was made with a slight inclination of the
head and shoulders, the feet together, side by side and the
knees straight. The lady's curtsy consisted of a simple bending
of the knees, with one foot carried back a short step, or placed
just behind the front, supporting foot; for ordinary occasions
the depth of the bend took the knee of the back leg about level
with the bottom of the calf of the front leg. The lady made her
bow with a slight, gracious inclination of her head.

When meeting a lady out of doors the gentleman removed
his hat, lifted quite off the head; if he was about to shake
hands with her the hat was removed with the left hand, but
when bowing to a lady in the street he raised his hat with
the hand farthest from her, in order to avoid concealing his
face. Gentlemen did not raise their hats to one another unless
there was a considerable difference in age or rank. When en-
countering a friend who happened to be accompanying ladies
with whom he himself was unacquainted, a gentleman raised
his hat as a gesture of politeness to the ladies, while looking
straight ahead, as the parties passed; to look at the ladies themselves implied that they were known to him. When a lady and
gentleman, who were only slightly acquainted, met in the
street, he awaited her recognition before bowing; this was the
English custom, but with Frenchmen and other Continentals
the recognition was initiated by the gentleman as being the
first to bow. Should a gentleman be on horseback when he met
a lady he knew, it was correct for him to dismount and lead
his horse. Thus the lady was saved not only 'the fatigue' of
looking up to his level, but also the 'impropriety of carrying on
a conversation in a tone necessarily louder than is sanctioned
in public by the laws of good breeding'. This observation calls
to mind some comments made by Aristotle: that the 'superior'
person did not appear to hurry, and had 'a deep voice and a
deliberate way of speaking', instead of being shrill in his tones
and excited in his manner. Similarly it was now said that
'there is a certain distinct but subdued tone of voice which is

peculiar only to well-bred persons. A loud voice is both disagreeable and vulgar'.

In the days when a horse-drawn funeral *cortège* proceeded along the street at a slow pace, gentlemen who were walking on the pavement removed their hats as the hearse passed them; the same gesture was made when walking or driving past the Cenotaph.

In the (often hatless) hurry and bustle of modern city life with its endless whirl of traffic, such sensitive old-time customs are mostly a fading memory.

Increasing informality supplanted the old formalities in many ways – even in small matters hardly worthy of comment, such as that 'between girls who know one another well, the bow becomes a smile and a nod, or on informal occasions a wave of the hand and a friendly word in passing'.

(c) HOSTS AND GUESTS

ETIQUETTE OF PAYING CALLS
Pre-war

Just after the turn of the present century ladies, it was said, 'stand upon strict and ceremonious etiquette with each other as regards both paying and receiving calls', and in the early twentieth century it indeed appears that they did. The impression received is of a feminine dominated world of fashion. The statement continues: 'Ignorance or neglect of the rules which regulate paying calls brings many inconveniences in its train; for instance, when a lady neglects to pay a call due to an acquaintance, she runs the risk of herself and daughters being excluded from entertainments given by the said acquaintance. When a call has not been made within a reasonable time, a coldness is apt to arise between ladies but slightly acquainted with each other. Some ladies take this omission good naturedly or indifferently, while with others the acquaintance merges into a mere bowing acquaintance to be subsequently dropped altogether.'

The first principle was that of knowing who should call upon whom. The established rule in this country was that those who had resided longest in a town or country place called upon those who had arrived more recently.

The formality of Card-leaving, which belonged to the etiquette of Paying Calls, followed special rules: 'The etiquette of card-leaving is a privilege which society places in the hands of ladies to govern and determine their acquaintanceships and intimacies . . . [and] is one of the most important of social observances, as it is the ground-work or nucleus in general society of all acquaintanceships. Leaving cards, according to etiquette, is the first step towards forming or towards enlarging, a circle of acquaintances'. Contrary to the etiquette of Calling where the residents of long standing called upon newcomers, Card-leaving was done by those who had just arrived in a place: 'Ladies arriving in town or country should leave cards on their acquaintances and friends to intimate that they have arrived, or returned home, as the case may be'. Cards for leave-taking were marked P.P.C. (*pour prendre congé*) in the lower corner and were left within a week or ten days of departure; it was permissible to send such cards by post instead of leaving them in person as for a social call.

The occasions for card-leaving were many: 'Visiting cards should be left after the following entertainments; balls, receptions, private theatricals, amateur concerts and dinners'. Princess Marie Louise, in her memoirs, confirms this, saying that 'visiting cards had to be left on one's hostess of the party, ball or dinner of the preceding evening', adding that she believed 'the leaving of visiting-cards has gone out of fashion, and a little note of "thank you" often accompanied by a few carefully chosen flowers, has taken their place'. It was not necessary on these occasions to ask whether the hostess was at home, except perhaps after a dinner party which was a more intimate entertainment. When enquiring after a friend who was ill, cards were left in person.

The correct time for Paying Calls was the next consideration. The usual ceremonious call was named a Morning Call although this was never made in the morning, the normal hours being between three and six p.m. It was said that the reason they were so named was that they were made before dinner; a tradition perhaps from days when the main meal (dinner) was served later than 1 p.m. A family living in the North of Scotland at this period was accustomed to sit down to dinner in the winter months at about 3, or even 4 p.m.

Calls were considered to be ceremonious or otherwise according to the hour they were made. If before 1 p.m. the call was a private affair between friends. It was said that 'from 3 to 4 o'clock is the ceremonious hour for calling; from 4 to five o'clock is the semi-ceremonious hour; from five to six o'clock is the wholly friendly and without ceremony hour'.

In the etiquette of Paying Calls, cards would be left on the lady only if she was genuinely out or said to be Not at Home, which was not the same thing and merely indicated that she was not receiving visitors that day, and did not imply any rudeness to callers. For the gentleman of the house, who normally would be away on business, a lady would leave cards on her social call.

If the lady-caller was on foot she would ask the servant who opened the door to her whether her mistress was At Home; if driving she could send her coachman or chauffeur to make the inquiry. The servant of the house would have been instructed as to her mistress's wishes; for her to rush off to inquire, leaving the visitor standing would give a bad impression of the household. If the lady was At Home the visitor entered without speaking again to the servant, who led the way ahead to the drawing-room, normally upstairs on the first floor. The correct procedure was for the servant to open the drawing-room door without first knocking and to step well inside the room in order to announce the name of the visitor. If the hostess was in the drawing-room, she rose to greet the guest, shaking hands. If, however, the room was empty when the guest was ushered in, it would be better manners, particularly if the hostess and guest were not well acquainted, to sit quietly instead of walking about (perhaps looking at books or pictures) and to rise when the hostess entered the room.

The visit generally lasted from ten to fifteen minutes and if after that time another guest or guests arrived, the first-comers could tactfully take their leave. It would be *gauche* to rise from their chairs the instant that the new arrivals were announced. While the hostess would rise always when greeting or bidding farewell to her guests, other ladies remained seated unless, it was said, the new-comer was 'of great social importance'. Whereas the ladies in the party remained

seated when any of the company got up to leave, gentlemen
rose to their feet if their hostess, in saying good-bye to her
guests, was standing.

As a guest was about to leave the room, the hostess would
ring the bell for her servant, who would escort the visitor to
the door and let her out, or be asked to call the visitor's
carriage (if the journey had entailed a long drive, the horses
were sometimes taken out of the carriage before the return
journey home). On leaving the room the departing guests
shook hands with their hostess and with friends and acquaintances. To those of the company to whom they had just been
introduced a slight bow sufficed, but it was no longer the
fashion to make any formal gesture to the assembled company in general.

Post-war

The rules of etiquette prescribed for pre-war years were
applicable during the Twenties, and many of the more usual
social courtesies have not changed since.

So long as households were able to maintain a requisite
number of domestic servants, social functions such as the
formality of Paying Calls mostly remained in fashion. The
etiquette surrounding this social duty remained much the same
as in earlier times. During Morning Calls, made in the afternoon, it was not customary for the hostess to provide food
or drink, though for some unexplained reason in country
places gentlemen might expect to be offered sherry; for ladies,
however, tea only was provided. If there were not many
visitors present the hostess might order tea to be brought in
on a silver tray and placed on a small table. Normally the
hostess poured out the tea and handed round the cups, unless
gentlemen were present to do the handing round including the
sugar and cream (or milk).

In the closing years of the Twenties protocol enjoined that:
'Now-a-days ladies do not stand upon strict etiquette with one
another with regard to paying calls', with the somewhat for-
lorn observation that 'people in society should have some
knowledge of the rules, even though they are no longer
strictly adhered to'.

The etiquette of calling was dropped only gradually, and in

the period when the older fashion was beginning to go out of date there could follow some confusion, as people were un-certain as to what was expected of them. In such matters definite rules make for smoother social contacts.

By the Fifties it was said that 'the custom of card-leaving is dead'. For one thing, in the often servantless days of this later period, the lady of the house would probably open the door herself to the callers, in which circumstance to present her with a card for herself would be absurd.

There remained, both then and since, other uses for cards (not counting Christmas cards), as when sending a gift or some flowers. The modern fashion of sending cards which contain appropriate messages for all kinds of occasions – birthday cards, get-well cards, Valentine cards and others – has grown considerably in recent years and seems to have supplanted the older habit of letter-writing.

Hostesses of the Fifties would not have expected their guests to leave cards after the entertainment to which they had been invited. Instead, it was polite to write a short note of thanks to the hostess, or after an informal party a telephone call of thanks was in order.

Should a lady wish to set aside an afternoon a week as an At Home day for receiving friends and acquaintances, she would indicate this on her calling card. As no invitations were sent out for the At Home, visitors calling of their own free will, the numbers who might turn up depended 'not a little as to the social standing of the lady who gave the At Home and upon the locality in which she lived'. Weekly At Homes which proved to be a social flop therefore were perforce dis-continued.

Opinions varied as to whether regular At Home days were the convenience that they claimed to be. It was said that 'the people who thoroughly enjoy At Home days are those who have more time on their hands than they know what to do with'.

BALLS AND DANCES
Pre-war

An invitation to a State Ball was issued by the Lord Chamberlain. A first-hand acount of a grand ball attended by

N

royalty is given by Princess Marie Louise. At one end of the ballroom the King and Queen and other members of the royal family sat on a dais; the King and Queen were provided with thrones and the royal princesses sat on gold and white chairs upholstered in crimson brocaded satin.

When the procession of the royal party entered the ballroom, the guests rose to their feet and remained standing during the dancing of the State Quadrille. This opened the ball and was danced by the princesses whose partners were Ambassadors and Cabinet Ministers, some of whom, being rather out of practice, had to be prompted 'and practically pushed through the various figures'. The dance over, the princesses returned to their elegant but not very comfortable gold and white chairs, and everyone present sat down again.

After this the band played the first waltz of the evening – 'invariably that enchanting Blue Danube'. Till the end of the First World War the dances which were in vogue were the waltz, polka, quadrille and lancers. At midnight, dancing was interrupted for supper. The royal procession was formed again, 'followed by the Corps Diplomatique, Cabinet Ministers, peers and peeresses of high rank', who proceeded into the State supper room, where there was a 'wonderful display of the famous gold plate' and a lavish feast of delicious food.

After supper the guests returned to the ballroom for more dancing, which ended with the Lancers at about 2 a.m. As the royal party left the dais, the National Anthem was played and they took farewell of the guests in this way: 'The Queen and the royal ladies made three profound curtseys, first to the left where the Corps Diplomatique were seated, then to the right where the peers and peeresses were seated and finally "en face" to the general company. Meanwhile the King and Princes bowed, also three times and in the same order'.

These were the days of the great London houses: Dorchester House, Grosvenor House, Derby House, Stafford (originally York and now Lancaster) House: all altered to become hotels, flats, clubs or for some official use. In them, it was said, the great hostesses of the Victorian, Edwardian and early Georgian eras entertained their guests. There were balls, receptions and large dinner parties taking place every evening in that brilliant London society of the last two decades of the nineteenth cen-

tury and the first of the twentieth. 'It was quite a usual occurrence to go to more than one ball the same night,' wrote the
Princess. Indeed, during the London Season a hostess who gave
a ball could have her trouble and expense spoilt by this fashion
whereby guests accepted more than one invitation and spent
their evening moving from one ball to the next. They would
arrive at the first engagement too early and stay for only a
short while; and their departure left the rest with a sense
that their remaining presence was due to their having 'no-
where else to go'. To avoid this embarrassment, hostesses who
felt themselves to be of a lower social standing sometimes
sought the aid of a lady of 'higher standing' to run the ball for
them; though even this was not without its difficulties.

A ball was a dance for a large number of people, perhaps
from 200 to 500, whereas a dance could be from 80 to 200.
Private balls of an exclusive nature were those given by the
hostesses of large houses and by Service or Hunt organizations
and the like, for which private invitations were sent. Admis-
sion to public balls, such as County, Charity, and Subscription
balls, was by ticket or voucher. In the eighteen-nineties fancy-
dress balls enjoyed immense popularity, mention being made of
a 'gorgeous' entertainment given by the Duke and Duchess
of Devonshire in their Piccadilly mansion. Those given at
Covent Garden were modelled more on Continental lines.
According to contemporary accounts, some of the examples of
fancy-dress chosen by the motley crowd were bizarre in the
extreme.

A hostess of a large private ball in Town stood at the top
of the staircase to receive her guests. A gentleman did not
offer his arm to a lady as they walked up the stairs, nor when
they entered the ballroom; the ladies preceded the men in
greeting their hostess and in entering the ballroom. The
hostess shook hands with all her guests when they arrived,
but it was not usual for the guests to take leave of the host
and hostess at large Town balls.

In addition to the dances named, the Washington Post,
Highland Reels, and sometimes (at a Country ball) Sir Roger de
Coverley were danced. Sometimes a London ball ended with
the Cotillon, which entailed the giving of expensive presents.
Princess Marie Louise tells of a gala entertainment given by

her husband (Prince Christian of Schleswig-Holstein) and herself in Germany, at which the Prince arranged a surprise for her: in the Cotillon, instead of the more usual baskets of flowers being brought into the room, a baby elephant from the zoo appeared carrying cotillon favours and flowers.

Country balls were felt to be more friendly affairs and the guests normally came in private parties arranged by a few ladies among their friends. Small gatherings for these occasions, such as a Hunt ball, would consist of house-parties of some ten to twenty-five people. The 'mamas, dowagers and chaperons' sat along the walls while 'the daughters unless they were dancing, stood by their sides'. This propping up of the wall by non-dancers, apart from being tiring, was responsible for the expression 'wallflowers' which could apply, it seems, at that time to men as well as to women.

Here the hostess stood by the door to the ballroom to greet her guests, the ladies entering first as in Town. London balls did not begin until about 11 p.m. but a country ball started at 9 or 10 p.m. and finished not later than 2 a.m. The ball was opened by the hostess or her daughter, who danced in the first Quadrille; this Quadrille took pride of place at the top end of the room farthest from the door into the ballroom.

In all cases of royal visitors attending a ball, these would be received by the host and hostess at the entrance to the mansion and conducted to the ballroom; on their departure the same procedure (in reverse) was followed. A guest would be introduced to a member of the royal family only by request of the latter; and should a lady be asked to dance by a royal guest, she would leave any converse to be opened by her partner.

Post-war

In the Twenties the procedure as given above for State Balls remained much the same. Foxtrots and dances of that genre had now replaced those of pre-war years: the Quadrille might still be danced, but the Cotillon with the giving of presents was seldom used. Etiquette no longer required that young girls should return to their chaperons after each dance.

Any ordinary ball or fancy-dress dance could be opened with a 'square dance', but this was no longer considered necessary; the usual practice was for the hostess and her partner, or for one of the daughters of the house, to take the floor first, after which all took partners and joined in.

Small dances in private houses were a popular form of entertainment, but by the close of the Twenties these had almost ceased to be given; the lack of servants made the preparations for the dance too burdensome and difficult for the host and hostess. Many young people attended dances organized privately, as by a tennis club, for which tickets were bought. Often the hostess arranged a small party and invited the guests to dine at her house first. If the party of dancers was of some size, or if in a country place most of the company present at the dance were acquainted with one another, so that in dancing all could mingle, dance-programmes were sometimes used, but the fashion for these started to be dropped when, as frequently happened, parties were composed of only four, six or eight people making programmes quite unnecessary.

The varied and often intricate steps of Foxtrots, Tangos, and other dances then in vogue, set a fashion till then unknown in dancing as a social pastime: couples found greater pleasure when dancing with a regular partner with whom they were able more easily to indulge their fancied steps. This led to their going to a dance for the purpose of dancing together the whole time. The *thé-dansant* in particular was popular with those who preferred to enjoy their dancing in this way. Couples could sit at small tables round the dance-floor, alternately eating and dancing, with little concern for other than the practice of their particular expertise.

OTHER ENTERTAINMENTS
Pre-war
The desire to get away from town and into the fresh country air provided the stimulus for outdoor entertainments which, though arranged with lavish care, retained a quality of simplicity. These outings enjoyed by members of well-to-do Society had nothing haphazard in their preparation. Sometimes they consisted of grand picnics for which invitations had been sent out, and were simply large luncheon parties held out of doors instead of indoors, and away from home instead of in the host's house.

Amongst what were claimed to be the more enjoyable forms were 'those well arranged little picnics given by officers in country quarters when the regimental coach conveyed some favoured few to some favoured spot'. For a friendly, small picnic party the spot would be chosen for its scenery, historic interest and so forth; the method of travelling there was normally by rail or horse-drawn coach. In those days it was possible to engage a saloon carriage on the train to take the party to their destination. The same service could be employed, if desired, as a convenient form of transportation for a large family to the place of their summer holiday. When arranging for a party to travel by saloon carriage it was expedient to order lunch at some nearby hotel; the cost being at that time from five to ten sillings a head. Or it might be that hampers of food were taken 'under the charge of one or two men-servants'.

A pleasant mode of travel to the picnic was by horse-drawn coach which could be hired, or driven by the owner of the vehicle. In this way the party kept together, whereas if they rode in separate carriages the tendency was for small groups to become segregated into, and remain in, cliques throughout the day.

Great quantities of food and drink seem to have been consumed, and if the party was large it was thought necessary to have one or two men-servants to arrange the table, to open the wine, and last but not least, collect and re-pack the plate, china or glass – even though the picnic was held out-of-doors. September was said to be the favoured month for these away-from-town outings so that a luncheon spread in the open was not without risk from the weather. This uncertainty could be safeguarded against if the meal was held 'in the best parlour of a rustic inn or, by permission, in a barn or shed'.

Another favourite summer entertainment was a 'water-party'. These were of various kinds, often given by owners of yachts, who invited friends and provided luncheon, tea and sometimes dinner on board. The party might land at some chosen place, but their main entertainment was on board the yacht. Sometimes a fair-sized party hired a yacht to take them to some pre-arranged destination where they were served with lunch and tea, the cost of which was shared by all.

Steam-launch parties were very popular, so were canoe parties either on the coast or on the river. After paddling the canoe, the party would land to make a fire and boil the kettle for tea; this was followed by 'the after tea ramble'.

Simpler outings for the family of ordinary country gentlemen included visits by pony and trap to friends and relations within driving distance. A favourite vehicle for the ordinary family was the governess-cart, for few families then possessed a motor-car. Families home on leave from the Colonies residing in the country with no pony or trap of their own were able to sometimes hire these, which were often the sole means of travelling any distance in these areas. Problems, however, could present obstacles, as in one case when the only available pony was that which pulled the village milk-cart; progress was erratic, as the animal could not understand why it was not allowed to stop at every house as usual on its daily milk-round.

Motoring, also, was not without trouble such as punctures, and the need to pause at the top of some steep hill in order to allow the car to cool down, the driver having also to reverse sometimes up a very steep gradient. The over-heating of cars at this time was so common that some of the older generation expressed their doubts whether motor-cars would ever be reliable enough for use in the heat of tropical climates!

Post-war

By the close of the Twenties, entertainments suggested for the amusement of country-house guests were of a more sophisticated nature than those of pre-war times. As part of this modern trend amateur theatricals, and the still newer vogue of private cinema shows, were popular with members of large country-house parties.

The production of an amateur play could sometimes be the *raison d'être* of a country-house party at an establishment of this kind where both space and money were not limited. In some of the large houses, small private theatres had been built and, depending upon the keenness of the host and hostess, the presentation of these amateur theatricals could achieve a high standard. A natural talent among the players plus a willingness to devote time and effort in rehearsal was of course essential, and to these values there was sometimes added the services of a professional stage-manager.

The cinema show also required a big house, for the screen needed either a large hall or, even better, a ballroom whereby maximum space for guests could be coupled with a minimum necessity for moving furniture about. The latest films were obtained from London and shown on the host's own projector. 'This new form of entertainment' we read 'has of late years become very popular in some sets of society.'

It soon followed that people began to possess their own movie-cameras and in some enthusiastic circles this led to the making of amateur films in which the guests now became screen actors and actresses. On a large estate scenes could be filmed in the park, on the lake, even perhaps with the inclusion of a private aeroplane, all of which could provide exciting 'incidents' for the story. Not only the rehearsals but the private viewing of the completed film could contribute to the guests' enjoyment.

SALUTATIONS. TECHNICAL DESCRIPTIONS

(a) THE SIXTEENTH-CENTURY BOW:

Draw the left foot backwards, the leg and foot turned outwards slightly, the knee straight. Keep the heels of both feet on the ground, with the body and head erect. Without pausing, bend both knees, simultaneously bowing the body forward from the waist. The head follows the line of the bowed body, without dropping the chin in towards the chest. As the knees bend, the weight of the body moves back partially on to the back foot, so that the weight is distributed evenly upon both feet. The knee of the back leg is turned outwards a little as the leg bends; if this is exaggerated the appearance is ugly. Throughout the bow the heel of the front foot remains on the ground. The heel of the back foot remains on the ground also, if the knee-bend is slight; if the bend is deep, the back heel is raised, keeping the weight of the body partially on the ball of the back foot. In a deep bow the back knee may touch, or nearly touch, the ground. On raising the body erect at the finish of the bow, the weight moves again on to the front foot, releasing the back one.

The above is a simplified version of the same bow described below by Caroso and Arbeau.

The Bow, from Fabritio Caroso's *Del Ballarino*, 1581.

'The slow (Grave) Reverence is made with the body well extended, also the legs; with half the left foot in front of the right, four fingers distant from it, taking care that the toes of both feet are quite straight. And since in the majority of Balletts there are eight perfect beats of music, or sixteen ordinary beats, let it be known that the entire Reverence begins and ends on the first four beats; . . . on the first beat one stands waiting with the left foot in front, as I have said, and with one's face turned towards that of the Lady; not as some dancers do, who keep it turned towards any bystanders who may happen to be there, in doing which they seem to slight the Lady with whom they wish to dance – she who must always be reverenced and honoured in every action. On the second beat the left foot must be drawn back in a straight line, so that the toe is beside the right heel; keeping it flat on the ground and not raising the heel at all; taking care, while drawing the foot back, to bow the head somewhat and also the body, performing this act with all the grace one can muster and keeping both knees straight. On the third beat the legs must be bent together with the body, the knees being moved somewhat apart, with grace. On the fourth and last beat, one raises oneself, bringing the left foot back beside the right, and raising the body and head together.'

The Bow, from Fabritio Caroso's *Della Nobiltà di Dame*, 1600.

(The Reverence, whether taken in 6, 4, or 2 beats, was always performed in the same manner, the number of beats merely indicated the speed and type of dance. Six beats were counted in certain dances in 3 beat music, and the 4 and 2 beats to common time – in those days named triple and duple time.)

'. . . the body being kept quite straight, likewise the legs, with half the left foot further forward than the right, so that the right toe comes just level with the left instep, the feet being about four fingers apart; taking care that the toes are kept straight, in the direction of the Lady, or whoever it be, whether one is dancing or not, and beware of doing as men generally do of letting one foot look at the Mediterranean and the other at the Alps, as if their feet were misshapen by nature; this is a most ugly sight. . . . When drawing back the left foot, take care to bring the toe level with the right heel, keeping it (the left foot) flat on the ground and not raising it at all; do not do it on the toe, nor draw it too far back, not too far to the side, as some are wont to do, who, by putting their knees too far apart, look as if they want to urinate; nor is it necessary to cross this foot behind the right, for all these modes are a most ugly sight to the onlookers. Having done this, you will gracefully bend the knees a little, and raise the left heel; and in drawing back the foot, you will draw the body back a little, spreading the knees somewhat, and in bending them you will keep the head high; . . . lastly you must raise yourself . . . bringing the left toe back beside the right instep.'

The Bow, from Thoinot Arbeau's *Orchésographie*, 1588.

'To make the reverence, you will hold the left foot firmly on the ground, and, bending the knee of the right leg, carry the tip of the toe behind the said left foot, taking off your cap, or hat, and saluting your damoiselle and the company, as you see in this figure. Having thus made the bow, straighten the body, and replace your cap, drawing back the said right foot, setting the feet together, so that the feet are placed one beside the other, as you see in the figure below.'

(b) THE SIXTEENTH-CENTURY CURTSY:

Beginning with the feet together, draw the left foot back a few inches behind the right, keeping the foot flat on the ground and the legs and body straight. As the knees bend, the body is inclined forward a little and, unless the knee-bend is very slight, the left heel lifts from the ground. The head is kept in line with the body, and not allowed to drop forward. Care must be taken to avoid putting the left foot too far back for it should not be seen protruding outside the hem of the skirt; the knees turn outward slightly when bending. The rise from the bend should be slow and smooth and, on ending the curtsy, replace the left foot beside the right. Although the feet do not separate very much during this Italian mode of making a curtsy, the backward movement of the left foot is the same as in the bow, so that the real difference between the bow and the curtsy is that, throughout the bending of the knees, the woman keeps her body more erect than does the man.

The Curtsy, as described in Fabritio Caroso's Della Nobiltà di Dame

'Firstly, she will learn to do the slow [Grave] Reverence in this wise, that is, standing with feet together, she must draw the left foot three or four fingers' breadths back, keeping the foot flat; then she must bend down and forwards, bending the knees, and the body a little and keeping the head straight, and immediately she has bent herself she will very gently rise up again, bringing the feet together in their place; and taking care not to do as some are wont to do, who first draw themselves back, bending the persons well, and then thrust the body forwards; so ugly an act that if I were to tell you what the movement resembled, everyone would burst out laughing. And certain others do it in another wise, bending well down very straight, and then raising themselves, so that they look just like a broody hen trying to sit on an egg.'

(c) SEVENTEENTH-CENTURY BOWS AND CURTSIES

from F. de Lauze's *Apologie de la Danse*, 1623.

i *The Bow made in walking and in passing by*

Remove the hat with the right hand, pass it into the left and hold it (the inside turned inwards) against the left hip in a negligent manner. If the bow is directed to persons on the right-hand side, on approaching them it is important to pause with the right foot in advance of the left. This last step, made with the right foot, should be performed slowly and deliberately to give those to whom the bow is directed an opportunity to observe that they are about to be saluted. The knees are straight, and the weight of the body is placed evenly upon both feet, which, together with the whole leg, must be turned outwards a little. Only the face is turned towards the company; the body does not turn. In this position the head and shoulders incline very slightly forward, whilst the knees bend a little, outwards over the toes. On rising from the bend, take the weight forward on to the front foot; this allows the left to move forward to resume walking. To make a bow towards the left-hand side, the left foot is placed forward before bending the knees.

ii *The Bow termed 'To salute a Lord or Lady'*

As above, the hat is taken off with the right hand, transferred, and held in the left. When near to those who are to be saluted, the right foot slides forward, slowly, about the distance of a short step. The legs and feet turned a little outward, and with both legs quite straight. The body is inclined slowly forward from the waist, without dropping the head forward; both knees bend outward, over the toes, though the knee of the front leg does not bend as much as does that of the back, which carries most of the weight of the body. The feet remain flat on the ground. The right arm is extended in a sweeping gesture forward and downward towards the ground, the palm of the hand uppermost. (The arm is not carried backwards behind the line of the body.) On rising from the bow, the hand is kissed to the person of quality, and allowed to fall naturally to the side of the body. It may be convenient to make the gesture of kissing the hand before the bow, but it must be made at the start of the bend and not at the finish. The weight is taken forward on to the front foot as the body rises. To assume an easeful position, if wishing to converse, a step sideways is

taken on the free (left) foot, the right foot sliding behind with
the knee slightly relaxed.

Comparing these last bows with those of the sixteenth century,
there are many similarities. In both, the feet are kept flat on the
ground, the knees are 'spread' or turned outwards, and the body
is bowed.

iii *The Lady's passing curtsy*

To make this curtsy, the lady waited until she was level with
those whom she intended to salute. The curtsy was then made in
the following manner:

If the person, or persons, are on the right-hand side, a quarter
turn to the right is made, in order to face them. This is done by
simultaneously turning to the right while taking a step sideways
on to the left foot, leaving the right leg and foot at the side without
weight on it. The right foot is then drawn in against the left,
before sliding it gently forward in front the distance of a short
walking step, while at the same time bending both knees slightly.
As the knees bend, the body inclines forward a little, and care
must be taken to keep the toes and knees turned rather outward.
The head must not drop forward. The curtsy is finished as the
weight moves smoothly forward on to the front foot, whereupon
the body straightens as the legs straighten. To resume walking in
the original direction, the body must turn back again by making
a quarter turn to the left. To do this, keep the weight on the front
foot, make the turn to the left while bringing the left foot forward
as in a walking step. The curtsy can be made, of course, to either
side. The turning of the body in this curtsy assists in sweeping the
train of the gown behind.

iv *The more respectful curtsy*

This curtsy was performed on entering a room where company
was assembled, when introduced to some one of consequence, and
when beginning or finishing a dance. Its origin goes back to medieval times, when women curtsied by bending the knees, the feet
placed side by side. In early days the knees and feet were held
naturally, without being turned outwards. In the seventeenth century De Lauze reveals that this was considered inelegant. By
'holding their toes together', he says, women appear very awkward.
When walking, ladies were taught to keep their toes somewhat
outward, and this applied also to the curtsy. Only country girls
and unfashionable women made bob curtsies, bringing the feet

together. The court lady was taught to 'direct' her curtsy in order to allow the recipients of her salutation to prepare their answering reverence. The means of directing the curtsy was achieved by a preliminary step taken to one side (right or left according to circumstances) at the moment of 'addressing' herself to the company. Having gained their attention, the curtsy then was made by drawing the disengaged foot gently to that which supported the body joining the heels only. The knees were bent smoothly, either slightly or in a deep bend depending upon the occasion, care being taken to keep the knees and toes outward. The body inclined only slightly forward. The arms open naturally and easily, falling to the sides as the bend is made. The wearing of heeled shoes enables the knees to bend in a deep curtsy without the necessity of lifting the heels off the ground. In the seventeenth century, when these curtsies were constantly performed, it was taken for granted, that if the situation demanded, the heels should be raised in order to make a deeper curtsy.

(d) ON THE SHAKING OF HANDS TO SIGNIFY A BOND

As You Like It: Act V. Sc. iv. (Touchstone' '– and they shook hands and swore brothers'.
Diary of Samuel Pepys (1662). 'After dinner comes Mr Stephenson, one of the burgesses of the towne, to tell me that the Mayor and burgesses did desire my acceptance of a burgess-ship, and were ready at the Mayor's to make me one. So I went, and there they were all ready, and did with much civility give me my oath, and after the oath, did by custom shake me all by the hand : so I took them to a tavern, and made them drink, and paying the reckoning, went away.'[1]

(e) ON REMOVING THE HAT. EIGHTEENTH CENTURY

'The manner of holding one's hat, removing it, and replacing it handsomely on one's head' (1745), was to be done in the following way : 'The grace of this action consists in disengaging the arm, without affectation, from above the thigh, carrying it extended for half the distance that it must make, afterwards rounding it as far as the hat, without any movement of the head; and to return the arm on the same track, with the same care.'[2] Instructions for the

[1] Samuel Pepys: *Diary*. 30 April 1662.
[2] Anon: *L'Art de la Danse*. Paris, 1745.

benefit of English youth (1762) are simple and explicit: 'If you bow to anyone passing by, do it in this Manner; raise the Right Hand to your Hat gracefully. Put your Fore-Finger as far as the Crown, and your Thumb under the Brim, and then raise it from your Head gracefully and easily.'[3] and in 1765 the movements are described thus: To uncover 'is done in three counts, the pauses between which should be imperceptible. On the first count, turn the arm outwards; on the second, raise it to the height of the shoulder and, on the third carry the hand to the hat, the wrist turned back, that is to say the inside of the hand visible. The arm is lowered in following the same principles. On the first count the hat is raised off the head; on the second, lower the arm to the level of the shoulder, the arm extended, and on the third it is lowered to the side, turned a little inwards'.[4]

(f) EIGHTEENTH-CENTURY BOWS AND CURSTIES

i The positions of the feet

Masters of the eighteenth and nineteenth centuries, in describing bows and curtsies, frequently refer to the positions of the feet. The five positions of the feet were identical to those used in ballet today, except that the feet were turned out less – the first position was one in which the toes made an angle of forty-five degrees from the line of the heels when the latter were touching.

ii The passing bow

This bow is a development of the corresponding bow of the seventeenth century. It is a pause in walking, and the difference consists in the manner of removing the hat, and of placing the front foot before bowing.

The hat is removed and held in the right hand, with the inside visible to those standing in front. According to whether the persons to be saluted are placed on the right- or left-hand side, the right (if they are on the right side) or the left foot moves gently forward on the toe with the knee well straightened. The forward foot is kept on the toe throughout the bow; this shows the lighter, more finished elegance of the eighteenth century in contrast with the more 'solid' posture of the previous period. To make the bow, the body bends from the waist (not the hips), or from what eighteenth-century instructions term 'the pit of the stomack'. The eyes are directed towards the persons as the bow begins and as

[3] Anon: *The Polite Academy*. London, 1762.
[4] Magny: *Principes de Chorégraphie*. Paris, 1765.

it finishes, and are lowered to the ground as the body bends. The right arm hangs easily at the side. The hat is *not* carried back beyond the line of the body, nor across the front of the body. As the body bends, the knee of the back leg is slightly bent, outwards over the toe of the back foot; the front leg is kept straight. In addition to bending, the body is turned from the waist towards the persons being saluted 'in a beautiful and agreeable Twist or Contrast sideways, looking upon the Person(s)'.

Towards the middle of the century another method for a passing bow was used 'to salute in passing, several persons at once', or when 'passing-by a lady of quality'. Here, 'the foot on which one makes the step which precedes this reverence should not be placed forwards as if one wished to continue walking. On the contrary, one must turn so as to wholly face the people whom one salutes and, without pausing thereupon, slide the [disengaged] foot behind to the fifth position'.[5] This last bow was made in the manner of the bow 'sideways' which follows below (iv).

iii *The bow forwards*

On a first entrance into a room where company was present, the man, having paused inside just clear of the door, with the weight on one foot 'in a graceful stand or rest', begins the 'bow forwards'. According to Tomlinson the foot without the weight was placed open to the side on the toe, and from there was 'scraped' forward on the toe to the distance of a short step in front, as the body and the back knee were bent. This movement took place to the 'counting of ONE'; the body was held for the 'counting of TWO in this respectful posture' and upon 'three' it was raised 'from this humble posture in one intire slow motion, till it stands erect on the . . . scraping foot'.[6] His version differs from all others merely in this forward scraping of the foot, for in the French examples this bow is no different from the passing bow with the foot forward on the toe, except that there is no turning of the body. Weaver ignored this bow and devoted his attention to that done 'sideways', which, as Rameau points out, was 'more ceremonious'.[7]

iv *The bow made to the side*

This more ceremonious bow was made quite differently from any

[5] Anon: *L'Art de la Danse.*
[6] Kellom Tomlinson: *The Art of Dancing.* 1724. London, 1735.
[7] Rameau: *La Maître à Danser.* 1725. Trans. C. W. Beaumont. London, 1931.

previous bow. In retrospect it may be regarded as the first 'modern' bow, for not only had it relinquished all trace of the early knee-bending, but it is separated from the modern bow by (literally) one step.

Just as the 'bow forwards' was so named because the leg placed to make the bow was moved forward, so this bow was so called because it was made by stepping sideways on to either the right or left foot, in this way : if to the right, the weight of the body is taken sideways on to the right foot the distance of a short step, leaving the left foot at the side, resting on the toe. Both legs must be quite straight, though the left leg should be somewhat relaxed, so that the left heel falls a little forward, allowing the inner side of the foot to be visible to anyone standing immediately in front. As this step is made the body is held erect, and the hat removed from the head (unless previously taken off). Without pausing, the back is then bowed, with no further movement of the legs, and *as* the body is raised again, the left foot slides gently behind to the fifth position. 'It is important to observe', writes a French master in 1745, 'that the bending of the body must be made in the pit of the stomach, in a manner that the back appears rounded; also that the greatest perfection of the reverence depends on the harmony which appears between the movement of the leg which slides and the bending of the body, which should be raised again at the same instant that the leg finishes its movement.'[8]

At the beginning and the end of this bow, Weaver says that the weight should be on the left foot, the right foot placed a very short distance diagonally forward to the right side, with the knee a little bent or relaxed.

Having made the 'bow forwards' with the right foot, this foot then moves sideways to make the 'bow sideways'. These two bows were made on formal occasions. If the hat was not to be replaced on the head it was held, after bowing, under the left arm.

Rameau remarks that some people drew the left foot behind at the same time that they bowed their bodies forward, which means that at the depth of the bow both legs were close together, in the fifth position, thus bringing the bow nearer to that of modern times. By 1797 what was named 'the ordinary bow for a young gentleman' was made with the feet held together (in the first position); thus bowing with the feet close together, instead of separated as in previous ages, gradually became the practice.

The bows just described are found in French treatises of instruc-

---

[8] *L'Art de la Danse.*

O

tion whose dates of publication span the eighteenth century (1725, 1745, 1765, 1767, 1787, and 1797). In them the terms used for the 'sideways bow' is *la révérence en arrière*, but in no case is there any suggestion of stepping *backwards*, the only backward move- ment being that of sliding the disengaged foot behind to fifth (or sometimes between fourth and fifth) position of the feet at the *end* of the bow, or of moving the foot backwards after the bow forwards to begin the bow sideways. The bow sideways was used not only on entering a room, greeting someone, or beginning and finishing a dance, but also when taking one's leave. 'Taking leave in Conversation', says Tomlinson, 'consists in Stepping aside, bowing and leaving the disengaged foot pointed sideways . . . during which it remains' (for the bow). 'And in the graceful Raising of the Body . . . it is drawn pointed, with the Knee straight, till it crosses behind the foot on which the Poise rests, and stands erect on the foot that is crosses behind, to be repeated as often as the Occasion requires.'[9] If the person taking leave was intending to make his exit to the right he repeated the bow always on the right foot, slowly edging away from the company.

v Locke. *On teaching children to bow.*

'*Manners*, as they call it, about which Children are so often perplexed, and have so many goodly Exhortations made them, by their wise Maids and Governesses, I think, are rather to be learnt by Example than Rules; . . . But if by a little negligence in this part, the Boy should not put off his Hat, nor make Legs [bows] very gracefully, a Dancing-master would cure that Defect, and wipe off all that plainness of Nature, which A-la-mode People call Clownishness. . . . Though the managing ourselves well, in this part of our Behaviour, has the name of *Good-Breeding*, as if peculiarly the effect of Education; yet, as I have said, young Children should not be much perplexed about it; I mean about putting off their Hats, and making Legs modishly. Teach them Humility, and to be good-natured, if you can, and this sort of Manners will not be wanting.' [10]

vi *The passing curtsy*

Tomlinson calls this a 'kind of walking curtsy'. Its similarity to the man's passing bow is confirmed by his observation that 'some Ladies make the Passing Honour the very same as I have described

[9] op. cit.
[10] John Locke: *Some Thoughts Concerning Education*. London, 1693.

for the Gentleman'; the only difference being that, in placing
the foot forward to the fourth position 'instead of bowing, they
curtsy to the right or left'. The lady makes the same turn of the
body from the waist as that made by the man, but in this case
she keeps her body erect. In this curtsy the lady bends the *back*
knee first, while moving the other leg forward to receive the weight
at the conclusion of the reverence. Another method, says Tomlinson, was to bend *both* knees at once, letting the weight remain
on the back foot, while the other moved gently forward the distance
of a short step, whereupon the weight was transferred to it.
straightening the knee. This method, he says, was used on entering a room, or when meeting someone.

The second method is the one advocated by Rameau, who adds
a turn of the body, by drawing back the shoulder nearest those
being saluted. He says that when saluting someone of superior
quality, the lady should use the more respectful curtsy (as follows
below).

A passing curtsy used to salute several people at a time was
also made and was similar to the man's passing bow of the same
date – 1745. Here, the step prior to the curtsy is made, not forward, but to the side, while turning to face the company, leaving
the disengaged foot pointed at the side; then this foot 'which
has not taken a step, slides in front to the fifth position' as both
knees bend for the curtsy. This bend – or 'sink' as it was then
described – with both the feet immediately under the body, instead
of being placed forward in the fourth position in front as in the
seventeenth century, enables the hem of the hooped skirts to rest
evenly on the ground during the bending of the knees, while the
knees themselves are quite concealed. In making these 'passing
honours' says Tomlinson, the lady must 'take regard as to the
Quality of the persons in the room'. She was to pay her respects
to all 'only as you meet them on your way'. In all her curtsies
the lady kept her body erect, making only a *very* slight inclination
of the bead and body. During the curtsies the hands remained
joined just below the waist, with the fan, if she carried one, held
in the right hand (Plate X*e*).

vii *The more respectful curtsy*

This was exactly the same as the corresponding curtsy made
in the seventeenth century. Called by the French masters *la
révérence en arrière* (as was the man's bow), it was preceded by a
short pause – to direct the curtsy – with the weight on the forward foot, let us say the left; then, moving the disengaged foot

(the right) sideways to the second position, the weight was taken on to it, and the left, sliding on the toe, was joined so that the heels only touched, the toes being well turned outwards. As the heels of the shoes worn were fairly high, it was possible to bend the knees quite low without raising the heels off the ground. For ordinary occasions it was inappropriate to make deep curtsies as this would have been considered affected. The hands remained either crossed in front (see above) or sometimes the arms fell easily to the sides. While dancing, the skirts were held at the side in each hand. On the bending of the knees (outwards over the toes), the body and head were inclined hardly at all from the perpendicular. As this was considered the more respectful curtsy, the depth of the knee-bend was more than that of the passing curtsy. The eyes were lowered on the bend and raised again to the person being greeted as the knees were straightened. To allow a foot to protrude from beneath the skirt at the back while making the curtsy, which happens if the leg is carried backwards as in a modern curtsy, was considered ungainly. In 1765 a footnote to the *révérence en arrière* says: 'One may finish with the feet in the third position but this requires more care and practice to avoid bringing one knee further forward than the other.'

The curtsy with the feet crossed in either the third or the fifth position, instead of side by side as in the first position, looks more elegant when the hem of the skirt is raised above the instep. This fashion was in vogue towards the end of the century, after the large hoop was discarded.

(g) NINETEENTH-CENTURY BOWS AND CURTSIES

i *The bow*

We have seen that, at any rate by 1797, the 'ordinary bow for a young gentleman' was made with the feet placed side by side. 'Placing himself in the first position,[11] the body erect, the arms hanging easily at the sides, without either stiffness or careless nonchalance; if he has a hat he will raise the right arm and, taking his hat in his right hand, will allow it to fall by his side, inclining his head, the chin touching the chest, and bending from the middle of the body, not from the hips, the knees straight; he will allow his arms to fall forward easily and without making them tense. On rising, the body, head and arms will assume the

[11] First position, as in ballet of the eighteenth century, the feet turned out to an angle of forty-five degrees.

posture they had before the bow, allowing the left foot to move to the fourth position behind' (i.e. the usual position of elegance when standing to converse).[12]

In 1838 the method is the same. The addition of a step to the side (then re-closing the feet to the first position), was the same as in the ceremonious 'bow sideways' of the eighteenth century. 'When the Bow is to be made ceremoniously, you step out with one foot to the second position and, placing yourself upon it, you draw, by a slidden step, the other close to it, in the first position; and then, resting on both feet, the body is bent straight forward a few degrees from the perpendicular line; the joints of the back are bent slightly outward, and by directing the eyes towards the feet, the head is brought down, and the curvation of the back is completed. The bow is now terminated by resuming your upright position; when, by fixing yourself firmly on one foot, you are enabled to dispose of the other in any requisite manner. When the bow is done upon ordinary occasions, the side step and slide are omitted, and you just bring yourself up in one movement into the *first position*, and then proceed as in the former case, only making the movements according to circumstances, less slowly.'[13]

By about 1860 the description, once so lengthy, becomes exceedingly simple: 'Bowing is merely a graceful inclination of the head and body from the waist.'

ii *The cursty*

This slight curtsy shows the development from the curtsy of the later eighteenth century, in which the foot was drawn behind to the fifth position. With the high heels worn in the eighteenth century there was no difficulty in bending the knees in this fifth position; but with the introduction of heel-less slippers in the nineteenth century, the foot, instead of closing in the fifth position behind, was taken backwards to the fourth. The curtsy begins with a step to one side, the weight of the body being transferred to this foot; the other foot slides, passing close to the supporting foot, by moving through the third position behind, continuing without a pause to the fourth position behind, diagonally across behind the supporting foot. As the foot moves, the knees bend.

[12] J. J. Martinet: *Essai ou principes élémentaires de l'art de la danse.* Lausanne, 1797.
[13] Barclay Dunn: *A Manual of Private, or Ballroom Dancing.* Edinburgh, 1838. p. 42.

The weight of the body remains on the supporting leg until the moving foot reaches the fourth position behind, when the weight is transferred onto it. The knees are straightened and the body is raised. The front foot remains on the toe, in order to continue walking. If the person wishes to remain standing, the front foot is drawn backwards, with the feet close.[14]

In 1838, 'in order to make the Courtesy formally', the same directions as those in the 1829 manual are given, except that these are more specific about the bending of the body. In former periods the lady kept her back straight, making only a very slight inclination forward. Now she curves her back. The bend of the body commences when the foot begins to slide near the supporting leg, and remains until the weight is transferred onto the back foot – 'when the spine is sufficiently curved, the body still curved, retires on the slidden foot, above which it is completely elevated, and the courtesy is finished'.

Exactly the same movements are described for the curtsy in 1860, the only addition being that, at the end of the curtsy, the weight of the body is transferred to the front foot, closing the back foot to the first position.

On ordinary occasions, the curtsy was still made in a similar manner to the 'passing' or 'walking' curtsies of the seventeenth and eighteenth centuries. 'On entering a room, for example, the lady sinks in the *first position*, and slides one foot forward to the *fourth*; she then bows, leaning slightly on the foot upon which she has sunken; and *with the body bent* she advances to the slidden foot, upon which she finishes her courtesy, by rising in the *fourth position*. On taking leave, and on some other occasions, the lady sinks, and slides *backwards*, bends the body as formerly, and retires to the slidden foot, on which she finishes her obeisance. These obeisances I would recommend to the attention of young people, as being a part of the forms practised in polite society.'[15]

[14] Anon: *The Young Lady's Book.* London, 1829.
[15] Dun: *A Manual of Private, or Ballroom Dancing.* pp. 43–4.

ETIQUETTE AND DEPORTMENT: NOTES

(a) *The custom of giving the right side* to the superior was an unbroken tradition from medieval times, as was the habit of walking a pace behind him.

> If thou serve a worthier man
> Than thy self thou art one,
> Let thy right shoulder follow his back,
> For nurture that is, without lack.
> *Urbanitatis, 1460*[1]

Walking with your master, in field, wood or elsewhere,
Do not walk even with him unless he commands you.
Boke of Curtasye, 1460[2]

'If the king walks with him, he will always go
a pace behind the king, and, when turning, he
should follow the laudable custom of the Spaniards,
which is to retire three steps backwards, and always
to put His Majesty on his right hand.'
F. Caroso, 1600

(b) *Whether the train of a lady's gown is carried by a woman or a man.*
From *A Book of Precedence* (mid-fifteenth-century). 'ffor it is accounted a higher degree borne with a woman than with a man'.

The twentieth century

'At the last two Coronations the trains of the Queen Consort and the Queen Regnant have been borne by six lady train-bearers who were of the rank of an Earl's daughter, or above. On both these occasions there was one lady who was the grand-daughter of of a Duke and each was given the rank, style and precedence of

---

[1] *Urbanitatis*, 1460. In *Early English Meals and Manners*. E.E.T.S. London, 1868.
[2] Also in *Early English Meals and Manners*.

the daughter of a Marquess for the day of the Coronation only. In 1953 Queen Elizabeth the Queen Mother's train was borne by the Queen's four Pages of Honour. In 1937 Queen Mary's train was also born by four pages in the Royal Livery and the King also had nine pages to carry his train. At the last two Coronations the trains of the Princess and Princesses of the Blood Royal were borne by their ladies-in-waiting.'

(Comptroller, Lord Chamberlain's Office, St. James's Palace, 25 May 1955.)

(c) *Three bows made to the king*
'. . . to White Hall Chapel, where Mr Calamy preached, and made a good sermon. . . . He was very officious with his three reverences to the King, as others do.'

(Samuel Pepys. *Diary*)

Three bows made by Ambassadors today when received in audience by the sovereign

'On entering the audience chamber the Ambassador takes one step forward and bows. He repeats this and bows a second time. Finally he advances to the Queen where he bows a third time. . . . The bow should be made in a normal way, i.e. a simple bow of the head without bending the body too far forward. . . . The Queen remains standing.

'The Ambassador is allowed to bring up to eight members of his staff, but these do not enter the audience chamber until the Queen has finished speaking with the Ambassador. The Ambassador is presented to the Queen by the Marshal of the Diplomatic Corps, who goes forward with the Ambassador and on his right side, while on the left side of the Ambassador is the Master of the Household. The Marshal of the Diplomatic Corps and the Master of the Household withdraw after the second pace forward, leaving the Ambassador to go forward to the Queen alone. With the Queen will be normally the Secretary of State for Foreign Affairs.

'The Letters of Credence are presented personally by the Ambassador when he reaches Her Majesty. No formal speech is made. The Ambassador finally takes leave of Her Majesty by shaking hands and bowing. He then withdraws a pace, but can leave the room with his back to the Queen. When, however, he reaches the door, he turns round to face Her Majesty before making a final bow and withdrawing.'

(Letter from Maj.-Gen. Sir Guy Salisbury-Jones, K.C.V.O., C.M.G., CB.E., M.C., Marshal of the Diplomatic Corps, Buckingham Palace. 27 May 1955.)

(d) *Estimate of a wardrobe, about 1860*
'There are four kinds of coats which [a man] must have: a morning-coat, a frock-coat, a dress-coat, and an over-coat. An economical man may well do with four of the first and one of each of the others per annum. . . . A man with £300 a year should not devote more than £30 to his outward man. The seven coats in question will cost about £18. Six pairs of morning, and one of evening trousers, will cost £9. Four morning waistcoats, and one for evening, make another £4. Gloves, linen, hats, scarves and neck-ties, about £10, and the important item of boots, at least £5 more. This I take it, is a sufficient wardrobe for a well-dressed man who employs a moderate tailor, and the whole is under £50. It is quite possible to dress decently for half that sum, and men of small means should be content to do so.'[3]

[3] Anon: *The Habits of Good Society*. pp 146-7.

SOME GESTURES FOR USE WITH THE FOLDING FAN

The following gestures have been selected firstly from Matthew Towle's instructions to a young lady,[1] and secondly from various attitudes to be seen in the drawings and paintings of the late seventeenth, and eighteenth centuries.

To Mediterranean peoples, the Italians in particular, the use of gestures to supplement speech seems always to have been a noticeable characteristic (see page 63); and with the introduction of the folding fan to seventeenth-century Europe, it was natural to incorporate this new toy into the established gesture-language of everyday use. Various actions used in handling the fan would become, in time, a kind of code by which it would be possible for ladies to communicate their feelings or intentions to admirers with whom, owing to the strict conventions of those days, it was not easy to converse freely.

Some of the meanings supposedly attaching to certain gestures with the fan have been included below, mainly to show how the fan may assist an actress not only to reveal a mood but to lend point to gestures characteristic of the period.

THE POSITIONS

First

This may be described as the ordinary, or normal position. The closed fan is held lightly between the tip of the thumb and the first (index) finger of the right hand, which is then placed in the palm of the left hand. When standing, walking, or making a curtsy, the hands are held thus at the point of the bodice, the arms somewhat rounded (see Plate IX*e* and X*e*). When seated, the hands rest in the lap in the above position.

Second

(*a*) Place the tip of the closed fan in the upturned palm of the

[1] Towle: *The Young Gentleman and Lady's Private Tutor*. London, 1771.

left hand, which is placed immediately below the right hand; rest the palm of the right hand, the fingers extended in a gentle curve, on the tip of the handle – the fan being vertical. The elbows are held a little away from the body in order to make the arms appear slightly rounded.

(b) Without moving the fan away from the hands, reverse the latter so that the left hand is now uppermost. This position can be used when either standing or when seated.

Third

The tip of the closed fan is pointed vertically downwards, so that it rests on the lap; the right hand assumes the same position as that in the Second (a), while the palm of the left hand is placed lightly on the back of the right hand, the arms rounded, as above. This attitude is suitable for elderly women – for example, Mrs Malaprop.

Fourth

The left hand rests in the lap, palm upwards; the right hand is placed in the left, with the fan held vertically in a half-opened position. The half-opened position of the fan is sometimes used to hide the face, as when praying in church.

ATTITUDES WITH THE FAN CLOSED

The tip of the fan is held against the face as follows:
(a)   To the lips. (*Be quiet, we are over-heard.*)
(b)   Touching the right cheek. (*Yes.*)
(c)   Touching the left cheek. (*No.*)
(d)   Lightly touch the tip of the nose. (*You are not to be trusted.*)
(e)   Touching the forehead. (*You must be out of your mind.*)
(f)   Rest the chin on the tip of the fan, held vertically. (*Your flattery annoys me.*)
(g)   Cover the left ear with the closed fan. (*Do not betray our secret.*)
(h)   Hold closed fan raised in front, and gaze at it with concentration. (*Make yourself clear to me.*)
(i)   Point tip of closed fan, held horizontally, towards the heart. (*You have my love.*)
(j)   Yawn behind closed fan. (*Go away, you bore me.*)

ATTITUDES WITH AN OPEN FAN

(a)   Hide the eyes behind widespread fan. (*I love you.*)

(b) hold the opened fan over your head. (*I must avoid you.*)

(c) Slowly lower the opened fan, in the right hand, till the sticks are pointing towards the ground. (*I despise you.*)

(d) With the right hand turned palm uppermost, extend the opened fan (like a plate) towards the persons. (*You are welcome.*)

(e) With the open fan held pointing downwards, the back of the hand visible to the person in front, make quick brushing-away movement. (*I am not in love with you.*)

INDEX
of sub-headings
and of
reference footnotes